P9-EJT-600

D0037782

BOTH OF US

RYAN O'NEAL

with JODEE BLANCO and KENT CARROLL

CROWN
ARCHETYPE
NEW YORK

BOTH OF US

MY LIFE WITH

FARRAH

All rights reserved.
Published in the United States by Crown Archetype,
an imprint of the Crown Publishing Group,
a division of Random House, Inc., New York.
www.crownpublishing.com

Crown Archetype with colophon is a trademark of
Random House, Inc.

Library of Congress Cataloging-in-Publication Data
O'Neal, Ryan.
    Both of us : my life with Farrah / Ryan O'Neal ; with
Jodee Blanco and Kent Carroll.
        p. cm.
    1. O'Neal, Ryan. 2. Fawcett, Farrah, 1947–2009.
3. Actors—United States—Biography. I. Blanco,
Jodee, 1964– II. Carroll, Kent. III. Title.
PN2287.O542A3   2012
791.4302'80922—dc23
    [B]   2012001731

ISBN 978-0-307-95482-4
eISBN 978-0-307-95484-8

Printed in the United States of America

The author and publisher wish to thank the Farrah Fawcett Foundation
and Redmond O'Neal for permission to reproduce copyright material.

All photos courtesy of the author, with the exception of the following:
page 139, courtesy of Oberto Gili; page 254, courtesy of Davis Factor/
www.davisfactorphotography.com; insert page 8, courtesy of Samuel
Lippke.

BOOK DESIGN BY BARBARA STURMAN
JACKET DESIGN BY LAURA DUFFY
JACKET PHOTOGRAPHS BY HERB RITTS

10 9 8 7 6 5 4 3 2 1

First Edition

THIS BOOK IS DEDICATED TO
OUR SON REDMOND,

who always will be our greatest achievement

and our best hope

AUTHOR'S NOTE

Everything here is true, although occasionally events may not be described in the exact order in which they occurred.

Play on, invisible harps, unto Love,

Whose way in heaven is aglow

At that hour when soft lights come and go,

Soft sweet music in the air above

And in the earth below.

—James Joyce, from "At That Hour"

BOTH OF US

CHAPTER ONE

BEGINNINGS

I remember taking her hand in the car, both of us joyous and laughing, the wind tousling those famous curls as we drove from Tahoe to Reno, to the church. The night before, someone had given me a Cuban cigar. I removed the gold band, slipped it onto her ring finger, and proposed. She accepted, saying, "So, you think you can make an honest woman of me, do you?"

The lake and the forest have a soothing beauty, magnificent nature in repose, almost as appealing to me as the ocean. Farrah preferred it there: the mountain air, the hikes, and, of course, the rugged horseback riding. It was one of those spontaneous moments when everything seemed aligned, as if nothing could get in the way of our future. We seemed perfect for each other. We had talked about getting married early on, but we were rebels. There weren't many people in the early eighties who lived such a public life who weren't married. We were getting pressured to do it, not by her parents, really, or by mine, but from society, so we finally decided to get hitched. Then the flat tire. I flagged down a car whose driver offered to take us on to Reno or back to Tahoe. He would have driven us to Cincinnati if I'd asked, but instead we chose the lake. We thought it was funny, even joked with each other that it had to be "a sign."

L ooking back, I can't help but wonder how my life with this rare woman might have been different if we had gone through with it that day. Why didn't I just fix the damn tire and get us to the church? Instead of finding a way to follow through with our plans, we let it go. We laughed about it for years. It wasn't the hand of God that flattened our tire that day. It was a lousy shard of glass.

Autumn, 1979

S he's married. Her name is Majors. I don't know her from Adam, well, Eve. Her husband is actor Lee Majors. He starred in a popular television series, *The Six Million Dollar Man*, and is also known for playing in Westerns. I know him. I first met him at 20th Century Fox when I was making *Peyton Place*, five hundred episodes at $750 per episode. That's also where I introduced, pointed out, Frank Sinatra to my costar Mia Farrow. I never played Cupid again. Lee is in Toronto for a movie and I'm there visiting my daughter, Tatum, who's shooting a film with Richard Burton. She's fifteen. Tatum and Lee run into each other, and Tatum says, "You know, I'm Ryan's daughter."

"Oh yeah, where is he?"

"He's at the hotel."

Next thing, he's calling me. "Come down and have a drink with me," he says.

So I do. And we get a little drunk together and decide to have dinner. Tatum joins us. Lee and I are both leaving the next day. I've been there a week. And he says, "Let's go home together. We'll take the same plane." He changes his flight. Lee is a companionable big guy, worth at least five and a half million. We fly home together and the limo drops us off at my house in town. It's on Tower Road, up Benedict Canyon and high in the hills, part of the old John Barrymore estate. We let the limo go and take my car. He lives farther up the hill near Mulholland on a street called Antelo Road, which has gates, and there's this beautiful girl waiting for him. She's delightful, full of childlike warmth. There is no pretense or cattiness about her whatsoever; she's vibrant and wholesome, refreshing in this town.

They kiss.

We play racquetball. They have their own court. And then she says, "Stay for dinner," which I do. She whips up this delicious meal of fried chicken with mashed potatoes and thick country gravy, a Texas treat. Farrah is so sweet to us. Lee's a heavy drinker, kind of a sad drunk. Their house is handsome, a tasteful blend of western-style accents and fine antiques. There are pictures everywhere, mostly personal photographs. Years later, an earthquake will destroy the place, and the cacophony of glass breaking, which frightened everyone, will turn out not to have been the windows but hundreds of photographs emerging from hundreds of frames. Lee takes me on a tour of the house. He shows me his closet. It's a room you can walk into, deep and wide. He must have seventy-five pairs of boots. *Where does Farrah keep her stuff?* I ask myself. We walk down the hall and he opens a door to a room you can barely turn around in. Farrah's clothing is piled in there. Some months later, Tatum and I will make the switch. Farrah's duds get the grand space. Lee's we move to his den.

I had gone to their home for dinner that first night, but the next night I was supposed to travel to Las Vegas for a boxing match. I have a friend, Andy "the Hawk" Price, who was fighting Sugar Ray Leonard. I'm a fight fan as well as an ex–amateur boxer. And Farrah says, in this lilting, ever-so-slight Texas drawl, "Well, isn't that fight on TV?"

I say, "Yes, it is."

And she says, "Why don't you see it here? You can play racquetball and watch it with us."

"Hm," I think, "hm . . . okay." I've just come back from Canada. I don't really need to get on another plane, so I return a second night. She greets me at the door with this winsome smile and says, "Aren't you glad you didn't go?" And that night there's drinking. She doesn't drink but he does. I drink a little. I'm watching them, and after dinner they start to talk about their relationship. I'm sort of encouraging them, saying things like "You're a wonderful couple."

He's a man of few words, a monosyllabic cowboy type. He's not naturally funny. Farrah is more natural, open, and she doesn't have any compunction talking about their problems. She says when they were staying in Nevada, he had a boat on Lake Mead. He was a TV star at this point, not the Six Million Dollar Man, but he was in a successful Western series with Barbara Stanwyck and Linda Evans called *The Big Valley*. It ran three or four seasons. This was before Farrah's fame from *Charlie's Angels* and the poster that had made her the fantasy of every teenage boy in America. Lee would call her from a bar near the hotel and say, "Get undressed, I'm coming home."

"So I'd get undressed," she tells me. "I'd wait for him, and wait for him. He wouldn't arrive so eventually I'd get dressed again." She says this more in resignation than bitterness.

"That's the kind of man I am," he responds. "You knew that when you met me."

I can see that the marriage is not the happy mating it once was. If reality shows had existed back then, this relationship would have been perfect fodder. The one I've agreed to do now with my prodigal daughter, Tatum, is alarmingly fraught. But that's all in the future. Back in the fall of 1979, I've just met the woman who will become the love of my life and I shouldn't be put off by that kiss I just saw Lee give her at the front door. I don't say anything. I just listen and then I go to my home in town, only a few blocks away. Two days

later, I'm at my house in Malibu, and Lee pops over for a
visit. We walk on the beach for a bit, and then he says, "Let's
go see Farrah."

"Where is she?" I ask.

"She's shooting a *Charlie's Angels*. She's at Disney
Ranch."

By this time, Farrah was no longer a regular on the
show. She had quit *Charlie's Angels* three years before after a
bitter dispute with creator Aaron Spelling over percentages
on merchandising. She wanted 10 percent, which is what she
had gotten for the famous poster, and Spelling wasn't about
to give in to her or the other Angels, so Farrah, in what was
back then a very gutsy move, left the series. Spelling sued
and it was settled out of court. As part of the settlement,
Farrah agreed to appear in four more episodes, one a year
for four years, one of which she was shooting that afternoon.
Although she was now being paid one hundred thousand
dollars for each of the episodes, compared to five thousand
dollars per episode when she was a regular cast member, she
didn't escape unscathed. Spelling Productions tried to have
her blackballed in Hollywood. It would take some time before the studios and production companies were willing to
take a chance on her again. But that was the Texas country girl in Farrah. It wasn't the money; it was the sense of
fair play. She was a stickler for traditional values, which ap-
pealed to me, especially after the unconventional women in
my more recent past.

Disney Ranch is a long haul on the 405 freeway. There is this huge back lot that productions can lease for location shoots. We drive out there about five in the afternoon and when we arrive, there she is on horseback. She rides beautifully, confidently, and she gallops over to us. We chat for a while and offer to drive her home. She has a scene to finish so Lee and I go into her trailer to wait. Once inside, he starts looking through her things, determined to discover some secret.

He doesn't mind that I see him doing this.

More evidence that everything isn't exactly perfect for them.

On the way back home—and this is when I get my first true sense of her—she's in the backseat, Lee and I are in the front, we're in my Mercedes, I'm driving, and I put on this tape of a musician I like named Ry Cooder. He's a wonderful guitarist and blues singer. As the music plays, she leans forward and I can feel her behind me, her clean, fresh fragrance, her aura, the warmth of her breath on my neck. I've known her for several days now, have experienced her at her most delicious, happy and smiling. I can tell that she likes me—she doesn't love me, she likes me—and she keeps moving in closer, and I get this helpless sensation. I didn't feel it with Ursula Andress or any of the other women from my past, but I do feel it with her and it's unnerving.

We drive all the way back to Malibu because Lee's car is parked at my house. I introduce Farrah and Lee to my fourteen-year-old son, Griffin, Tatum's brother. He's thrilled at the chance to meet the TV star whose poster is a favorite among his friends. It's evening now and we decide to have dinner nearby at Orsini's. Now Lee drinks and pees all the time, so he's constantly getting up and leaving the table, which gives me long moments with Farrah. I try to be funny, and then mix in some anecdotes from my years in television. I just get rolling, and he's back. "Here, Lee, have another beer." He's gone a long time, must be standing there like a plow horse. While he's relieving himself, Farrah talks about throwing him a surprise going-away party at their commodious house in the hills. He's departing for Canada again in several days to start a movie with Robert Mitchum, and I, selflessly, volunteer to help.

We finish dinner and go back to my house. By now, I'm nervous. Lee drives a Porsche and he's been drinking all night. As I'm watching him and Farrah climb into this sports car and drive off, I say to myself, *I hope he's okay to drive.* Looking back now, I shudder because I didn't take his keys and insist they spend the night. Thankfully, they arrived home safely.

Farrah's party for Lee is a big success! She's a relaxed host. She puts people at ease. The vittles are surpassed only by the interesting guests. It's an intimate group: Robert Mitchum, whom I've admired and secretly envied ever since I saw *Out of the Past,* the best noir film ever, and his son Jim, with whom I'd attended University High; singer/songwriter

Paul Williams and his wife; Jack Palance and his daughter. Farrah is wonderful and we tease each other and flirt. We've initiated something. It seems to me we're obvious but no one, including Lee, seems to notice. The only thing that keeps it from being a perfect evening is the absence of my daughter. Tatum is still in Canada making the film, but I've been regaling her over the phone about my dinners with Lee and Farrah. She's electrified, can't get enough. I remember that a few years back, Tatum and I were staying at the Pierre Hotel in New York, and she overheard the bellman mention to someone that Farrah was also a guest. My daughter camped out in the hotel lobby half the night waiting for a chance to meet her. They never connected. Maybe this should have been a premonition of things to come, but of course none of that occurred to me at the time. Tatum had always gravitated toward sophisticated women, cool characters whose chic exteriors did little to hide their neuroses. When I dated Bianca Jagger, she became Tatum's fashion model. Tatum even emulated her characteristic hat and walking stick when she went to the podium to accept her Oscar as Best Supporting Actress of 1974. She was ten. And Ursula Andress never minded Tatum slipping into bed between us. Ursula thought it sweet. It worried me, but I allowed it to go on. I guess I recognized that Tatum was the primo female of the house, a role she would be loath to relinquish to Farrah.

. . .

Lee's now back in Canada, phones me, implores me to call Farrah, make sure she's okay. "She's all alone up there," he says. "Why don't you take her to dinner one night?" I swear I can't believe it. "Don't worry, I've got Tatum here in Toronto," he adds, thinking he's being witty. A week goes by. I don't call Farrah. I feel uncomfortable about it. Lee's an okay guy and she seems susceptible to any emotional offer; plus I don't want to look like a predator. I hold out, hoping maybe she'll call me. She doesn't. As I'm leafing through the newspaper I notice an ad: "Santa Monica Civic Auditorium Sunday night Ry Cooder." A reason to call. That's all I need. I pick up the phone and dial. She answers.

"I thought I'd hear from you," she says, with more self-control than I can muster.

"Well, I have a reason to call you now. Your husband asked me to take you to dinner. I will if you'll see Ry Cooder with me."

"Can I call you back?" she asks.

Not what I want to hear. Who does she have to get permission from? I'm intrigued as it's usually the women who wait by the phone for me to call and not the other way around. She does phone me later in the week as promised and says she'd love to go. In the interim, Swifty Lazar, the talent agent, invites me to a party he and his wife, Mary, are hosting a couple of days before the Cooder concert. He always has memorable parties, lots of famous people, very famous people. And I think, *I wonder if Farrah would like to go to that? Do I want to push it?* So I call and tell her who'll be there: Gregory Peck, a fine gentleman and almost as suave as Cary Grant; Ann and Kirk Douglas; Burt Lancaster; and other stars of that era.

"Is it dressy," she asks?

"No, no," I reply. Well, of course it is but I badly want her to go, and I don't want her saying to herself, "Oh, do I have to buy a gown?" Farrah is not a gown person. Not yet. She arrives at Lazar's fabulous home in jeans and boots and a snakeskin jacket. She sparkles in jeans, exquisite, but everyone else is wearing bespoke suits and couture dresses. It's an older crowd, and she's miffed that I hadn't made it clear to her what people would wear. To my surprise and delight, she's the hit of the party. They're fascinated by her. She's famous because of *Charlie's Angels.* And, of course, her poster. But she's not well known to this group. They recognize her. They just don't know her. I watch this room full of the truly illustrious gathered around her while Swifty asks her questions and Kirk Douglas tries to get her attention by broadening his smile till we can see his molars. She's quite taken with the attention. Farrah, I should realize, is an icon of young American womanhood. I don't fully grasp that at first. I worked with Streisand. Now she's an icon, but of a different sort: a woman who conquered the entertainment business by sheer force of will and talent. When we were shooting *What's Up Doc?*, Barbra had "kill approval," meaning she had the final word on which still photos the studio could use in its publicity and marketing campaign. That's harder to get than final cut. I remember sitting there with her, watching her review these thick stacks of photos one at a time . . .

"Gee, that one looks good, Barbra."

"Kill it."

"But I like—"

"Kill it!"

"Barbra, it's hard to achieve the perfect shot, and I look good in that one!"

"Nope, nope," she'd say, flicking one discarded photo after another onto the floor.

She's never satisfied with how she looks. But that's not unusual in Hollywood. Some of the biggest stars carry the most burdensome insecurities. One of the few people I know who is consistently self-confident is Ron Reagan, now Governor Ronald Reagan, who's announced his candidacy for president. He's likable. He's an effective governor under difficult circumstances, but I don't think he's president material. He has the actor's gift of making a speech and he looks the part, but the economy is still shaky and the cold war is in a deep freeze. Washington is a hell of a lot bigger than Sacramento, and I'm not sure what's inside that brown suit. I worked with Nancy way back, 1959, in a *General Electric Theater* production. She played my mother. He was always on the set supporting her. Today, years later, thinking about them reminds me of what Farrah and I had.

Farrah and Barbra will meet at the house of my agent,
Sue Mengers. Sue is a powerhouse, represents Barbra and
many other luminaries of the time: Burt Reynolds, Cher,
Joan Collins, Michael Caine, Sidney Lumet, my former director and former friend Peter Bogdanovich, Herb Ross. Sue
is married to director Jean-Claude Tramont; Barbra was the
maid of honor at their wedding. There's a party every weekend at Sue's house, always with a wonderful cast. Sue makes
an effort to ensure that everyone's at ease. Her Bel Air home
is lavish, reminiscent of Hollywood's golden era, and invitations to her soirees are coveted. In the movie business, films
are packaged and Sue is a wizard at the game. She's the one
who gets the producer to buy the script that's written for her
actor client, who only works with a director who's another
client of hers, or some such tangled maneuvering. I bring
Farrah to one of these parties. Gore Vidal is there, and he
and Farrah talk about the movie based on his novel *Myra
Breckinridge*, which she was in with Raquel Welch, the only
woman I can think of whom Farrah ever had a problem
with. (Once, at an event, Raquel complimented Farrah on
her beautiful white teeth, then added demurely, "Of course
all the ones in the back are yellow.") Rod Steiger, who always seems to be doing an imitation of himself, is there;
so too are Tony Perkins; Neil "Doc" Simon and his wife,
Marsha Mason; Jack Lemmon, who, as usual, plays the
piano without being encouraged; Walter and Carol Matthau.
Some years back, Walter had made the film version of *Hello,*

Dolly! with Streisand. They didn't get along. Walter was famously quoted in an interview, "She has no more talent than a butterfly's fart," a comment neither chivalrous nor accurate. It's a star-bright evening. Maybe it's best that Barbra isn't there. Jack Nicholson arrives late after the Lakers game. We talk politics with Warren Beatty, Gene Hackman, Blake Edwards and his new mate, Julie Andrews. My instincts are liberal, like most of the people I know, maybe because we can afford to be. But we have problems here that no one wants to be honest about. Southern California is not the paradise it was only a dozen years ago. You can't see the mountains most days for the smog, and the 405 threatens to become a parking lot rather than a freeway. A guy I know told me about the Central Valley farms and the Mexican migrants who used to be seasonal. Now they don't go home after the harvest. Who can blame them?

I remember another gathering at Sue's, which would happen later, after Farrah and I have been long together. I'm agitated that night because Mickey Rourke is monopolizing Farrah. He isn't coming on to her, just keeping her to himself. I'm actually jealous. Farrah notices, leaves Rourke, grabs my arm, and says, "Come with me." She marches me up the stairs to a bathroom and, without bothering to even lock the door, straddles me on the toilet and makes love to me. "Feel better now?" she says. I certainly did.

When Sue asks to manage Farrah, she whispers to me, "She'll be as big as Streisand." Barbra sees the future in a different way. When she meets Farrah at another of Sue's gatherings, her casual comment about our relationship is "I give it three weeks."

But now, at the beginning, the night of the Lazar party, I wonder: *What's with this Texas girl, this poster beauty with a wonderful tenderness who doesn't seem affected at all by the tumult of pop stardom?* We hesitate, then finally kiss for the first time. She is a great kisser. She has such sweet breath. I knew by the way she was kissing me that she had made up her mind.

JOURNAL ENTRY, OCTOBER 9, 1979

I'm still in a state of tranquility. Could this be love? I mustn't do anything to harm it. My little family needs someone of grace and goodness. Farrah and I talked and kissed till past 3 a.m. (no real lovemaking yet). She said that since the moment Lee left for Canada she's been desperate to see me. I was stunned. This woman has kept herself in check for many years. We give each other strength and hope. Being fair to Lee is not the least of our problems. When I am sure, I'll tell him. Tate will be both puzzled and thrilled. She's never really found a girl she could turn to, confide in, be a sister.

Reflecting, I remember the insecurity that would take hold of me while waiting for her phone calls, worrying I wouldn't be able to hold on to this extraordinary creature. She once told me, with a wink and a smile, that she was maybe the most recognizable person in the world, and I said, "What about Muhammad Ali?" She answered, "Well, okay, the most recognizable Texas girl in the world," and we both laughed because it was true. Imagine the pressure of loving someone whom millions of men fantasize about and desire? Imagine trying to be that woman and having to live up to your own poster. They would be obstacles we'd both struggle dearly with. But I don't know any of that now.

JOURNAL ENTRY, OCTOBER 10, 1979

This is the part I hate most. The waiting. All right, she called and Lee had been on the phone with her from Canada for that long hour. She's concerned about him, trying to be decent. I admire her more and more. Now I'll dress nicely and go to see her. She's sad about her situation. And while I occasionally feel a wave of guilt, I keep telling her she is in fact a happy woman and she should act like it. No tears. I can make something out of her and she me. A kind and generous Catholic girl with morals and clear thinking. I'll disrupt that but only in part. I quite like it in her.

Two nights later, we see Ry Cooder. I take her home and we make love for the first time. She has her period and she's

shy because she thinks it might offend me. I tell her that I've
never been as excited.

JOURNAL ENTRY, OCTOBER 11, 1979

Tonight I'll take her to dinner, tomorrow the fights,
Friday J. J. Cale and Saturday the beach, followed
by a Dave Mason concert. Dave called today and
asked me to come. I wonder if she's up to such a full
schedule. She's an exciting lover, at once innocent
and uninhibited. There is no one in my life to
compare her to.

Went to my jeweler today and found the most
beautiful garnet ring. It turns out to be her birth-
stone. Maybe I'm crazy for such impulsive actions
but this feeling is so rare and delicate that I tend to
be excessive, at least a little bit. Besides her natural
allure, there's a dignity that is bewitching and dis-
arming. She smiles with aplomb. I'm a lucky guy.

Lee is not happy. He has a right to be sore. Farrah tele-
phones and says he's been talking to her from Montreal
and that he's clearly upset she went to a party with me. He
doesn't deny telling me to call Farrah. He just didn't think
I'd go out with her. Later he relents and admits that he did
suggest I take her out but that he didn't think I'd actually
do it. Who *wouldn't* go out with her? I feel like flying with
her to the moon, to borrow a lyric patented by Sinatra. All

this turmoil makes her sad and slightly hopeless. I'm ready to call him myself. She wants to wait for a decent and delicate way to confirm that the marriage is over, but I doubt that's possible. That part of her life has become disheartening. When she's with me, she's a different person, happy and full of cheer.

As the days become weeks, my relationship with Farrah deepens. I'm like a schoolboy, calling her every day, telling her how desperately I love her. I'm forever bringing my darlin' flowers, surprising her with little presents, spending long, lazy nights making love. This earth-daughter has touched me like no other woman before her. Our blissful romantic bubble will be punctured by reality soon enough, but for now, I'm luxuriating in every minute of this feeling.

I'm not the only one who's been struck with Farrah fever. My sons Griffin, fourteen, and Patrick, twelve, adore her too. Griffin is Tatum's younger brother from my first marriage, to Joanna Moore, and Patrick is from my second marriage, to Leigh Taylor-Young, both actresses. I get the boys every weekend. Patrick is serious and respectful. With Grif, you never feel that one day he'll be a model citizen. He is already defying authority at every juncture, whether in school, on the playground, or with me. He has an angry wall around him that seems to become more impregnable every year.

I have a sauna at the beach house, and Farrah loves to take saunas. The boys start hiding under the bench in the hopes of getting a quick peek, but she's always running so late that by the time she finally gets into the sauna, they've been poached and have to be pulled out and doused with cold water. Farrah is always patient with them and kind. I'm especially pleased for Griffin, who can use all the attention and affection he can get. His and Tatum's mother, actress Joanna Moore, has battled addiction and depression all her life, and it's damaged the children.

I know it's only a matter of time before I'll have to face what I call the third-date conversation, which I've managed to avoid until now. You know what I'm talking about: that meaningful exchange every woman who's starting to fall for a man inevitably initiates, in which she wants to know more about his exes and his children. Not my favorite subject, but at least I'm ready for it when Farrah finally asks. We're curled up on the couch watching reruns of *Peyton Place*, and she shyly admits that she was a fan of the series and used to have a crush on me. I admit not so shyly that I saw a few episodes of *Charlie's Angels* and entertained a thought or two of my own about her. "Tell me," she says. I do and she actually blushes.

As we're confessing to our mutual attractions, there's a scene with Leigh Taylor-Young on *Peyton Place*. Farrah is watching in earnest, then turns to me and says, "How long did you know her before you were married?" I tell her it was only a few months. "Why so fast?" she asks. I decide to skip the details and get to the heart of the matter. "Because she was pregnant and I was still a good Irish Catholic boy under the sway of his parents' morality." Farrah looks perplexed, then says, "But isn't that the same thing that happened with Joanna Moore?"

"Pretty much," I respond. "I felt responsible and I was too young to know any better. The difference with Joanna is that I wasn't married to anybody else when we got together."

"Do you mean you were still married to Joanna when you started to see Leigh?" she says.

"Technically, but the marriage was already over." I'm trying to be honest here without incriminating myself.

"Did you love them?" she says.

"I did love Leigh and I tried to convince myself I loved Joanna."

Fortunately, Farrah's best instincts kick in.

"That must have been really hard for you," she replies. "Knowing about your marriages makes me feel better about what happened with Lee, and now I get why you've been so understanding about him." I say to myself, *That was easy.* Then, as if on cue, she says, "But what about the children? It must have been tough on them." I take a deep breath and explain. "Patrick's fine, and I think will stay that way. It's been much more difficult for Tatum and Griffin, but now that she's with me full-time and Grif is here on weekends, I know they're going to be okay. And professionally, Tatum is already on her way and Griffin may be even more talented, so both could have big careers." Farrah doesn't press me, but I sense concern and a certain knowledge that we're going to have this conversation again. But in that moment, I really did feel confident about my children's futures, especially now that Farrah had entered our lives. In all honesty, it did occur to me that there could be problems, but I swatted them away like gnats, not wanting to spoil the moment. Entire relationships are built on moments like these and I didn't want to waste this one. Farrah takes my hand and holds it to her cheek. Then she says, "I'm here to help you. I've never been a mother. You may have to guide me."

I tell myself this is a wonderful woman. Now my children and I can have both ends of the rainbow.

Though Farrah and I don't flaunt our affection for each other in public, and by now Lee, who's still in Canada, has acknowledged our union, we both know that soon the tabloids will start commenting, and we're lucky it's Liz Smith, the doyenne of New York celebrity gossip, who first reports on us in her column in New York's *Daily News*. She calls it "a very real love affair," and the item is tastefully written. I bet Sue Mengers fed it to her. That's Sue, always working an angle. She probably figures the publicity will increase our price. The papers continue to follow us but the coverage is rarely hostile; in fact, the reporters keep referring to us as "handsome together," and they repeatedly hint at a love affair, which it certainly is. The only real rough spot is a piece in *People* magazine that suggests what Farrah and I share together is tawdry and inappropriate, but we get through it. While part of me is bursting with pride that this fair-haired goddess actually loves me, another part feels bad about all the publicity because it's humiliating for Lee. Though I want nothing more than for each of us to be open about this love life of ours, and not let the world learn about it through the tabloids, it would be heartless for Farrah and me to rub it in Lee's face by declaring publicly how much we love each other.

JOURNAL ENTRY, NOVEMBER 1, 1979
Starts slowly for both of us. The sun is already
warming our old souls. The beach has never been
so appealing to me. We ran and threw Frisbees,
and played with our pups. Farrah brought her dog
Satchel with her today. It makes me feel young when
we're together. Christmas is beginning to draw near
and so I'm trying to get it organized properly and
with these new additions to the family it becomes
ever more complicated. And there's the question of
where Lee will be.

Reading these journal entries today, I marvel at my determinedly frivolous judgment. And to be fair, everything really did seem okay. I was in love and very, very distracted.

By now, Tatum is on her way home from Canada and all I've been hearing on the phone from her is how delighted she is that Farrah and I have found each other. Lee has never mentioned anything to her. She even hints that we should marry if Farrah divorces Lee. So I decide to surprise my daughter and take Farrah with me to the airport to pick her up, thinking she'll be thrilled. I'm wrong. After our telephone conversation, I'm surprised that Tatum seems uncomfortable, defensive. All of a sudden, it's almost as if she's the jealous other woman. I begin not to trust Tatum with Farrah. Tatum is too talkative around her. I had known a few women. Tatum had been around them. Some she liked, some she didn't. Not that there were hundreds, but there were a few and I'm still friends with most of these women. It's out of respect for them as well as for Farrah, who knew about my past, that I don't feel comfortable discussing my previous relationships. For somebody who's been the center of an avalanche of publicity for fifty years, I live an unusually private life, always have, and I'd be a traitor to one of my few guiding principles if I changed now. And so the next day I plead with Tatum, "Please, let's not remind Farrah. Let me be this virgin that she's found, let me keep the illusion alive just for a little while." Tatum will have none of it. One day, several months after Tatum's return, Farrah and I are in the car, and she points to a street corner we're passing and says, "That's where your daughter told me about you."

"Oh, really, what did she say," I reply, slightly sick to my stomach.

"How hard you are on women, that you're not always a nice man, that I should be wary of you."

These were the ways that Tatum, who was living with me, tried to undermine my love affair with Farrah. She couldn't help it. She suspects mixed motives because everyone in her life has always had mixed motives.

I knew what was happening with Tatum: she was angry and confused. I just felt powerless to stop it. I was spending more time with Farrah than with her, and she saw it as a betrayal, that I was abandoning her. I adored Farrah, and felt I deserved this chance at happiness. In my defense, when Farrah came on the scene, Tatum was pretty independent, had her friends and her life, and didn't need me like she did when she was a little girl. And so, to me, it didn't seem that I was spoiling the situation. I was just happy with Farrah. Alas, the happier I was with Farrah, the less Tatum appreciated it. She believed I was withholding something from her and giving it to Farrah. Tatum and I still retained our daily routine. We'd run or take long walks on the beach. If either of us was up for a part, we'd read each other's scripts. It was the evenings that were different. Tatum was no longer my regular dinner companion nor did she accompany me to parties. The evenings belonged to Farrah now. That was tricky for me, and I can't say that I handled it particularly well. I wasn't sophisticated enough to know what to do to get over this hump. I had a habit of making molehills out of mountains. I had allowed my daughter to become too close to me and now I had somebody I wanted closer.

Farrah reacted in all the right ways, which moved me deeply because I suspected, even though she never said anything, that Tatum unnerved her, that she was afraid of her. Farrah was so loving and supportive, continually reassuring me, "It's okay, we'll see more of her." She'd encourage me to bring Tatum with us to the movies, to dinner, anything to try to break through. Tatum turned sixteen on November 5, and we had her birthday party at Farrah's, at the big house in the hills, and invited all her friends, including Michael Jackson, Melanie Griffith, and Andy Gibb, who was one of Tatum's great crushes. I was upset when he died, so young and so mysteriously. As best I recall, at the party the kids kept listening to Pink Floyd and the Rolling Stones. They didn't play pin the tail on the donkey or spin the bottle. But I saw the way Tatum was looking at Andy and I think they played something called "Truth or Dare," a game I didn't understand then and don't now. The Diane Keaton look from *Annie Hall* made its appearance on two or three of the girls. The only thing I remember about the boys is that they all wanted to get close to Melanie.

I give my daughter not one but two cars—a brand-new BMW and a classic MG sports car. I had them brought to the front of the house. Each had an enormous ribbon with a bow tied around it. The entire party escorts Tatum outside. I expect an ordinary teen response from her, a squeal, a little jumping up and down, a big hug for her old man. Instead there's nothing. She just looks at the cars and then at me. I can't tell whether she's confused or disappointed. "Thanks, Dad," she says as she turns and walks back into the house. By this point it's clear I'm not going to able to console my daughter with fancy presents. The stronger Farrah believed in me, the less Tatum did. When I met Farrah, I felt that she was a godsend and that my only daughter would agree. It wasn't fair assuming my daughter could think like an adult. I had treated Tatum as if she were a grown-up since she was nine, not a healthy approach to a child. Farrah can only enhance us, I thought then, which under normal circumstances should have been the case.

I now realize "normal" had long since been an impossibility for Tatum and me. I truly believe that if Tatum and I had not made *Paper Moon*, she would be dead, because she would have been with her mother and she wouldn't have had the escape route that I gave her. She would have been a teenager in that erratic life with the worst of all adult behavior to imitate. First, I saved her, made her my whole world, and then I pushed her out.

I remember once, out of frustration, actually trying to explain to Tatum: "You're asking me to choose the girl I don't sleep with. You can't ask that of a man. You're missing one of the chief ingredients of a relationship. I love you, you're my daughter, but there are certain aspects of my life you cannot fulfill." The words came tumbling out of my mouth before I realized what I'd said. I'd inadvertently complicated our relationship. It was utterly inexcusable. I was blinded by love and in my naïveté I expected my child to sympathize with me. I kept telling myself that everything was going to be okay, that we could step blindly into that blue yonder of the faultless American family. Except there was already too much spoiled fruit on the family tree.

My mother saw what was happening and understood I would have to leave Farrah to get Tatum back. My mother didn't want to say that. She also knew I wouldn't do it. Both my parents did. My dad, Blackie O'Neal, was a well-known screenwriter and my mom, Patricia, a respected if occasional actress. They were familiar with the impermanence of Hollywood relationships. They knew my first two wives, and saw Farrah as an oasis of calm and responsibility. They also realized that the more I fell in love with her, the more Tatum would retreat. It might have been different had I enforced healthier boundaries beginning with the filming of *Paper Moon*, where father and daughter were equal partners, but we acted like adult friends, and it would prove our undoing.

But at the start, Farrah and I are still confident things will work out with Tatum, so we're concentrating on building our life together. Also that November, trouble is brewing on another front. Lee calls from Canada with an apparent change of heart and tells me to stay away from his wife, or else. I tell him I can't do that because I love her. He repeats, "Stay away from my wife and stay out of my house!" We hang up and my adrenaline is pumping. I share this news with Farrah, who says that Lee wrote her a note about how I am only after publicity, trying to exploit her fame. He has no clue how much she means to me. He calls me back the next day, I suspect prompted by Farrah, to apologize for threatening me. I can see why Farrah was once in love with him.

F arrah and I go to New York together before Christmas. She has some personal appearances scheduled for Fabergé shampoo; she's their spokesperson, and I decide to tag along. We would make one of our lasting memories on this trip. I've booked us into the Pierre Hotel, on Fifth Avenue overlooking Central Park, my favorite hotel at the time. After we unpack, I tell Farrah, "On the top floor of this building there's a deserted ballroom, and all the plaster of Paris cherubs that must have been on the ceiling are now just lying on the floor." The Pierre was about to undergo an extensive renovation. I see her eyes light up with angelic anticipation.

"Let's have a look," I say. "We have to take the elevator as far up as it will go, and then climb a staircase. I don't think we're allowed up there, so we'll have to sneak around."

"Let's go," she whispers. We do and we find the cherubs. They must weigh twenty pounds each. And there she is, bending over, picking up these ornaments, and trying to balance them in her arms. I have the flashlight.

"What are you doing?" I ask.

"That one, and that one," she says, pointing. "Oh, there's another good one behind you!"

These are not tiny keepsakes, mind you, they're big and heavy, each one like a miniature chubby Buddha. We take as many as we can carry downstairs and then have the bellhop deliver boxes that we pack with our loot. We take four home with us and they remained in our family room for years. I still have one at my beach house. Farrah and I would often reminisce about this trip—her struggling down that flight of stairs making loud banging noises as she wrestled the fat, unwieldy statues. That was my image of her forever: hunched over, sweating and laughing, moving those things in the dark. For years I would imitate her, bending over, pretending to be carrying something enormous, trying to get down the stairs with too many cherubs.

Though I smile looking back on Farrah's formidable display of physical strength that day, she wouldn't always have such vibrant health. Worrisome things would crop up from time to time that would be successfully treated and go away. But back then, neither of us gave them a second thought. We were young and full of life, eager to begin our future together.

The first of these scares comes right before our first Christmas together, in 1979. Farrah develops a group of benign cysts on her breasts, six of them, that must be surgically removed. (Over the years, she'll end up having many more.) She goes home to Texas for the procedure. While I stay in LA at her request, Lee reasserts himself, racing to Houston to support his wife, and then returning with her to

LA to nurse her back to health. It's clear that Lee is making a final attempt to win her back and she's too weak and too tired to resist his caretaking. Though I'm deeply annoyed, Farrah keeps reassuring me that our love is safe.

JOURNAL ENTRY, JANUARY 5, 1980
Lee has gone to Houston and has returned home with her. I'm hurt and confused. Farrah called and said not to worry because she loves only me. Not very consoling when I know they'll go back to the same house and with the captive eye of her mother, who's come with her.

JOURNAL ENTRY, JANUARY 6, 1980
My girl is back but can't talk to me because Lee is in the house and watching her closely. Why is he still there? I spoke to her briefly and she sounded conflicted. I have lots of questions for this girl. Definitely not yet my idea of an independent woman, although I recognize her sense of propriety. She still feels an obligation to Lee, but is not sure how to honor it. I'll be patient with her. It seems I have no real choice short of firing her before she fires me.
   She finally called. It was sweet, but slightly hurried as Mr. Majors was in the shower. I was abrupt and she quickly called back pleading for understanding and professing never before finding

**love as she has with me. I believe her and it made
me feel relieved.**

It turns out Farrah's mother will not soon be my ally. Lee doesn't stay at the house long. He's doing a movie and has to go back on location, so now Lee's gone, and I'm here in Los Angeles. I meet Pauline for the first time. She's staying with Farrah until she's fully recuperated. She has a very deep southern accent. She's a quarter Choctaw Indian, high cheekbones, an older woman but striking. She's strong and stoic, not at all impressed by Hollywood fame and glamour. She's been the one sturdy constant in Farrah's life and Farrah depends on her for advice and emotional support. Farrah also has an older sister, Diane, who lives in Texas. She and Farrah, though loving sisters, share few interests and so they seldom chat. Diane sometimes helps Farrah with PR, without ever breathing the air of Southern California. Her doing Hollywood PR from the Lone Star State always amused me.

I'm up at the house with Farrah. Lee's moved out and they've filed for divorce. We're watching television in her bedroom, and the doorbell rings and it's Jay Bernstein, with his fiancée. Jay's a too slick character. He was Farrah's manager for a while until she finally gave him the boot because he treated her like a dull-witted child who also happened to be a meal ticket. He managed Suzanne Somers too. Farrah told me how Jay used to think nothing of doing her newspaper and magazine interviews, telling the stunned reporters, "You don't need to talk to Farrah because I know exactly what she would say." Jay had always been close to Farrah's mother. He was smart. Flowers on her birthday, that sort of thing. And he was always working the mother because he knew Farrah listened to her. So Pauline had some affection for him. Farrah lets him in the house with the fiancée, and I can hear them going into the kitchen, already arguing about late, unreliable financial reports. Farrah sounds furious. I'm still in the bedroom. There's this long hallway with photographs lining the walls, and I hear Pauline saying to the fiancée, "And this is Farrah when she was three years old, and this is her when . . ." Suddenly there's a terrible crash in the kitchen. I bolt down the hall, go flying past Pauline, who keeps on pointing out pictures to this woman, ". . . and this is Farrah making her first communion," she continues, never even looking up, as if this sort of thing happened all the time. As I run into the kitchen, Farrah is throwing a frying pan at Jay. Now these are the kinds of frying pans you have to grip with two hands. I yell, "Stop, you'll tear your stitches." It's a lethal throw that fortunately misses. I say to the man, "I don't know how you riled her but you better go before she picks up another pot."

It's my first glimpse of Farrah's temper. I've been careful so far to keep that part of me disguised. I try to tell myself that truly passionate people are like that; it's what makes us who we are.

I want to win Pauline over, so I take Farrah and her to Chasen's, and invite my mother to join us. Farrah always loved Chasen's chili. Fred Astaire is in the entranceway when we arrive; he escorts us to our table and does a few dance steps, a dazzling start to our evening. There are lots of show business people and everyone is extremely friendly. Chasen's is the gathering spot for Hollywood's elite. Hitchcock is there that night. Though dinner goes well, and both mothers are polite to each other, it's hard not to see that they have nothing in common. My mother is cultured and Pauline has a third-grade education. Don't get me wrong: Pauline isn't dumb by any stretch, but she's limited. She also has no interest in show business whatsoever, thinks Farrah should come home to Texas. I can tell Pauline doesn't like me. I think it's because she doesn't approve of Farrah's being involved with another man before she's divorced. She never does warm up to me, though Farrah's dad, Jim, and I will become the best of buddies in the coming years. We share an interest in history. On the way home from Chasen's, there's a program on the radio about Lord Mountbatten. The women are dozing, so I listen. The IRA assassinated him in Ireland, blew up his sailboat with him and his young grandson in it. I'm all for the reunification of Ireland, but can they only get there by killing?

After Pauline goes back to Texas, Farrah is still in pain. At the time, I owned a house in Big Sur. Lee is still on location with the movie. I decide to take Farrah there to heal.

We take the Pacific Coast Highway, the PCH, driving along some of the most magnificent vistas anywhere in the world. Hours later, we're winding through the mountains, it's late at night, an enormous storm hits, and we get caught in a rock slide. As I'm trying to weave through, we're trapped by a huge boulder in the middle of the road. Suddenly, fearless Farrah, with her chest still full of stitches, opens the door, steps out of the car into the torrential rain, and says, "Help me move that thing!" I reluctantly get out and together we start pushing. I can feel the mud rising up past my ankles. Then there's another stranded motorist flapping his arms at us, screaming, "Landslide, landslide, get out of there, are you crazy?!"

"Honey, they're saying we're crazy," I shout against the pounding rain, hoping she'll retreat to the car.

"Just keep pushing," she says. "We can do this."

After a few tries, we're able to move the damn boulder enough to squeeze the car past it.

The rest of the ride, thankfully, is uneventful.

Big Sur is both soothing and exhilarating. Henry Miller used to live nearby. He would send everyone notes at Christmas, telling the recipients the presents he wanted. He once asked me to buy one of his own books for him. Later he would be ensconced near me in Pacific Palisades with his Japanese wife, who, I'm told, never stopped nagging. Henry told people she may have thought she had married a rich man. He was only famous.

JOURNAL ENTRY, JANUARY 10, 1980

We relax slowly and soon she's cooing and then the comedy of me fumbling around trying to enclose us from the Big Sur night. She giggles till she falls asleep and I lie next to her with great expectations in my heart, for she is beginning to endear herself to me. Next morning, I shower with my girl, a fine way to kiss and cuddle.

JOURNAL ENTRY, JANUARY 14, 1980

So far it's a little bit of heaven. We've had a relaxed evening by the fire with Van Morrison playing in the background. We talk at length about assorted problems like husbands and wives. Lee is packing at their home as I write this, probably for the last time.

We talked long into the night and finally slept. That we are still together amazes me. I guess it's because I'm just not used to having such a pure beauty like her and it still makes me wary. I feel a lot of powerful urges and I want to make sure that I act only on the good ones. I'm sorry we're leaving so soon tomorrow, but it's been very fulfilling in a lot of ways. Especially to me. We talk because there's no TV, no movies, a chance to get to know each other. I do want to go all the way with this.

JOURNAL ENTRY, JANUARY 17, 1980

Our last day in this magnificent seascape surrounded
by ancient cliffs and trees, we shop at a bakery
with irresistible smells. The drive home to LA is
exhilarating. Three weather changes and all the
colors the sky affords and I'm riding with my own
rainbow. Straight to the heart. I felt Farrah slip
out of bed early this morning, so I went to join her.
I want to tell her stories, dance around the room
to Stephen Stills, and then take her to lunch at the
Brown Derby. A sad spot was the call from Tatum.
She's fought with her mother again. I listen to her
story and know it's beyond me. I turn to Farrah
for help.

Farrah's visibility is on the rise. She's shot another cover
for *Vogue,* is completing the last of her *Charlie's Angels* appearances, which she'll be talking about with Barbara
Walters, and she's beginning to get some interesting made-
for-TV movie offers. Meanwhile, my career is in a slump.
The follow-up films after *Paper Moon,* including the entertaining comedy *The Main Event,* with Ms. Barbra, did
nothing to bolster the industry's respect for my acting. But
the great lost opportunity was *The Champ.* A huge success,
it made Ricky Schroder a star and revitalized Jon Voight's

career. That could have been Griffin and me. I was cast as the father, Griffin was promised the son's role, but the studio changed its mind about him so I walked. I was proud of how my son dealt with such a severe disappointment. He took it much better than I did.

And now I'm reading the script for *The Hand*, and Sue Mengers is convinced I'll get an offer. I've also been given the script for *The Thornbirds*. In the end, I won't get either role. Michael Caine will be cast as the lead in *The Hand*, and *The Thornbirds*, instead of being a film, will be turned into a television miniseries starring Richard Chamberlain. I want to work, but the offers aren't coming. I find myself increasingly interested in Farrah's career, which is at a turning point. She wants to extend herself but doesn't know what form it should take. This is where I see an opportunity. If I can't help myself, maybe I can help Farrah by bolstering her confidence. She doesn't realize what her gifts are, thinks they're just her hair and smile.

I've come to believe that a lot of love is about admiration. Farrah has some acting licks. For one thing, she can read a scene and own it, just read it once and know the lines word perfect. All she needs now is the chance to play a role that has nothing to do with beauty. The opportunity arrives that spring of 1980 with a made-for-TV movie called *Murder in Texas*. This is a true story about a doctor with a mistress who loses interest in his wife and slowly poisons her to death—the wife, not the mistress. We pull Farrah's hair back into a ponytail. She has these tiny ears that are adorable; they're endearing. We downplay her makeup and wardrobe, and voilà, the actress emerges. She's brilliant in this part, so believable. It would mark the beginning of many similar successes. I enjoy coaching her, helping her run lines and hone her craft. I've surprised myself.

This was the love I had not known before. I had known the kind of love that children have for their parents, but that's expected; this was very different. Since my marriages, I'd practiced serial monogamy. I liked smart, unpredictable women, such as Anjelica Huston, but I never fell in love and I had no intention of getting married again. Farrah and I enhanced each other in ways I'd never experienced. I grew up a Catholic, but I had fallen away. I had two ex-wives when I met her. You're not supposed to get divorced in the Catholic Church and I did it twice. I didn't have a parish; I didn't have a priest whom I could speak with. Farrah wasn't lapsed. I started going to Mass again because I could accompany her. We'd get dressed in our Sunday clothes and go to Mass together every week.

It's the spring of 1980 and for me a season of endings and beginnings. Farrah's divorce from Lee enters its final stages. She has to buy him out of the house, but at least he's gone. He knew the marriage was over and eventually allowed their uncoupling to be largely amicable. And Farrah and I are free. We're launched. I've won Farrah. I've lost my daughter. It's as if Tatum has moved to a very strict boarding school that doesn't allow telephone calls or visits from parents. A letter a month at most. This girl was a chatterbox as a child. We'd exchange 1,000 words an hour; 950 came from her. There's this emptiness in my life now; that musical voice, that comforting background presence that helped make my house a home is gone. My old Catholic soul finds it ironic that Easter, the season of renewal, is just a week away. Tatum never blamed Farrah. She blamed me. That spring, Tatum moves out of the beach house into an apartment in Beverly Hills, across the street from her mother, who is dangerous for her, a complex and bitter personality still struggling with addictions and depression. I enjoy my wine and an occasional toke, and have for years, but I have never known the hell of addiction. It will be twenty-five years before my daughter and I will reconcile. And now all of America will be able to watch us struggling with our history on a reality show . . . dear Lord. I'm doing this because Oprah is a friend and Tatum needs a job. These are not career decisions; they're about repaying a loyal supporter and soothing my ancient anguish of having lost my daughter more than two decades ago.

CHAPTER TWO

CHARLIE'S ANGEL
AND MINE

There's a famous 1981 photo of Farrah, Tatum, Griffin, and me at a Rolling Stones concert that's always reminded me of an Ultrabrite toothpaste ad. It was the first picture ever taken of us together, the proud single father with his beautiful girlfriend and his talented, adorable children, arm in arm, laughing and happy, a perfect image of what was becoming a new version of the modern American family. I remember the photographer introducing himself and then politely asking my permission before he snapped the photo. While such respect from a paparazzo was not commonplace then, it would become even rarer in the months and years ahead, but I wasn't thinking about any of that then as the four of us smiled for the camera. It was a glorious day.

Farrah has just finished shooting *Murder in Texas*, the first movie in which she's recognized as a serious actress. It was shot on location. I visited the set as often as I could. Though my own schedule is hectic, my career isn't what it once was, but Farrah's is about to ignite and I want to contribute to her growth and success. She responds well to my coaching and it solidifies us as a couple. I soak up every sweet moment. It's also more rewarding than trying to restart my own career. Though I'm getting work, the scripts are medio-cre and the films forgettable. When my old friend Freddie Fields offers me the lead in a movie he's producing called *Rambo: First Blood*, I turn it down. I tell him it's because I don't think the role is a good fit for me, which though it may be true, isn't the reason. I don't want to leave Farrah. Between you and me, and this is not an easy thing for a man to admit, there was always a part of me that was afraid that if I was away from her for too long, I'd lose her. It turns out to have been the right decision. Sylvester Stallone does an effective job. Though I do wonder where my career might have gone had I told Freddie yes.

At the time, my mind is elsewhere. I feel most alive whenever I'm on set with Farrah. The energy of our col-laboration is exciting and constructive. I remember a scene in *Murder in Texas* in which she has to sing, and she's ner-vous; so I tell her to throw her leg up on the chair like Mae West and belt it out. It works. Her nervousness transforms into moxie, and if you look at the scene closely, you can see the moment it all clicks. Though I try to be subtle whenever I'm on set, usually communicating my suggestions through a series of hand signals that we'd devised, every so often it causes a problem. One time a director will attempt to have me removed. At Farrah's insistence, he'll be replaced.

Around this same time, Farrah has also completed work on the screwball comedy *Cannonball Run* with Burt Reyn-olds. I'm not there. I know Burt well and I expect him to make a play for her, but surprisingly, he doesn't, not until he casts her in *Butterflies Are Free* at his theater in Florida. She tells me that one day he's climbing all over her and he says, "I know Ryan, he's great, he's funny, but if somebody pulled a gun on you, Ryan wouldn't throw himself in front of the bullet, but I would." So I say to her, "Now wait a minute, why would someone be shooting at you; what did you do? Besides, maybe good old Burt has a point. He can sacrifice himself. Why should both of us have to take a bullet?" I make light of it for Burt's sake as well as for my own. He's a friend. I know that he honestly can't help himself and who could blame him? When the situation was reversed, I wasn't able to resist Farrah either.

Though both of our schedules are challenging, often putting us on opposite coasts, we seize every opportunity to be with each other on location. While I'm doing the action/adventure movie *Green Ice* with Omar Sharif and Anne Archer in Mexico, near Acapulco, Farrah visits during a break from *Cannonball Run*. The day she arrives, I'm doing a scene in which I'm being chased out of a club. The bad guys are gaining on me and I'm running toward the beach. I dive into the water and start swimming out to sea to avoid capture, at which point I'm being filmed from a helicopter. The pilot is hovering low to provide the cameramen a good angle. The propellers on this bird are powerful; they're roiling the water and making waves and I can feel myself being pulled under by the swell. I keep waving my arms and yell-

ing. The director gives me a thumb's-up from the cockpit.
I'm breathing in more water than air and I can hear these
gurgling sounds coming out of my mouth. "More!" he signals. I see him gesturing for me to "go broader!" I nearly
drown by the time they figure out I'm not acting. There's a
photo of me coughing and sputtering in Farrah's arms. It's
embarrassing. The whole enterprise ends up being an em-
barrassment. Though working with Omar Sharif is a joy.
He's touched by Farrah's warmth and sincerity. A genuinely
kind man, several years later when Farrah and I are in Paris
and she's hospitalized with a bad case of food poisoning,
Omar is very helpful to us both.

Omar is also a wonderful raconteur. One evening over
dinner after we've wrapped for the day on *Green Ice*, he tells
Farrah and me about meeting Rita Hayworth for the first
time. This happened long before he was a star, when he was
a young actor from Egypt and new in LA. Hayworth takes
a liking to him at this party and says, "Do you have a car?"
He'd hired a car and driver for the evening so he answers yes.
"Then you may take me home," she says. She lives high up in
the hills of Beverly and it's a long, dark drive through steep
winding roads lined by dense foliage. Omar keeps telling the
driver to slow down. In Egypt, the houses aren't perched on
the edge of cliffs. When they arrive, Hayworth turns to him
and says, "Dismiss the driver." He gladly obliges. They go
into her house, an exquisite bungalow beautifully furnished.
It smells like gardenia and woman. Now he's wearing a tux-

edo and she's in an elaborate gown so he's delighted when she politely excuses herself to slip into something more comfortable. While she's out of the room, he begins to take off his tux. He's down to his boxers and obviously excited. She emerges in loose pants and a gray sweater. "What are you doing?" she says. "Is that what you thought?" And she escorts him out. This is decades before cell phones and he has no way of contacting his driver to come back for him. He walks home. Omar had been led to believe that women of the California variety were straightforward and understandable. He'd obviously been misinformed.

Rita Hayworth was suffering from Alzheimer's long before anyone knew what it was. I remember being at a party at David Selznick's when he was married to Jennifer Jones. It's a formal dinner. There are about sixty of us, and I'm seated next to Rita. There are wine decanters on the table so I offer to pour her a glass. "Ms. Hayworth, which would you prefer, red or white?" She tries to answer, but her speech is so hesitant I'm not sure what she's saying. Everybody around us thought she was drunk, but she never had a single drink. I listened to her the rest of the evening. I didn't have to hear what she was saying. I just kept looking into those beautiful eyes, grateful and happy merely to be there.

Rita represented a Hollywood era when the major studios ruled. If you were an actor, they reinvented your past to suit their publicity machine, they defined your present by assigning you films, and they held your future hostage because without a studio contract it was almost impossible to get work. While people of extraordinary talent and irrepressible personalities such as Bette Davis fought back—occasionally to her detriment—actresses such as Rita and Myrna Loy flourished in the system. I would have been perfectly happy with a long-term studio contract, but some guys from my era, such as Warren Beatty and Peter Fonda, natural-born independent filmmakers, would have revolted.

That same year I make *Green Ice,* I have to be in New York for three months to shoot *So Fine,* a comedy for Warner Brothers with Jack Warden and a wonderful Italian actress, Mariangela Melato. Farrah wants an apartment with a sauna, so I find this place on Fourteenth Street, a loft, that has both a sauna and a Jacuzzi. We live there while I'm shooting the film. My ex-wife Joanna Moore is in no shape to care for Griffin, who's sixteen, so we take him with us to try to get him into the music school at Juilliard. We realized it was a stretch for a drummer but we wanted the best for him. By this point, Griffin has been in and out of numerous schools, exhibiting many of the same behavioral problems as his mother, and I'm worried for his future. But at the time, all I wanted was for my boy to be able to pursue his dream of becoming a professional musician. Though Juilliard doesn't accept him we're able to find him a music tutor while we're there. It's a wonderful time for us. Griffin and Farrah like each other and she gives him all her support. Farrah so wanted to love my children and have them love her in return, and the more Tatum withdraws, the more Farrah tries to funnel her love to Griffin and Patrick. Griffin doesn't always make it easy. Patrick glows from her attention.

Farrah loved New York pretzels, the ones street vendors sell out of carts. They cost fifty cents back then and she would always keep two quarters in the front pocket of her purse so if she wanted to buy one she'd have exact change ready. One day, Griffin steals the fifty cents and, boy, does she ever chew him out! An old friend also visits us during that time. I've known him since high school. He had gone to prison for smuggling pot. When he gets out, I hire him to be my assistant, what we now call a handler, and to do stand-in work for me. Years later, Tatum will skewer him in her memoir *A Paper Life*, accusing him of everything from supplying my family with drugs to molesting her. To this day, my daughter and I disagree about my friend. But back to the early eighties in New York with Farrah . . .

The media continue to track us. The divorce is still not finalized and we're trying to maintain our privacy for everyone's benefit. It proves impossible and eventually comes to a head the night Farrah and I are meeting Tatum, who's flying in to see Richard Burton on Broadway in *Camelot*. Tatum had recently starred with him in the film *Circle of Two*.

Farrah and I have on our fancy best. We're leaving the Pierre Hotel, where we've stopped to see some friends before the show, and paparazzi are swarming the entrance. I'm holding a bottle of Coke. We make our way through the throng of photographers and get into the limo. It won't start. The driver gets out to check the engine and a bunch of thugs with cameras jump into the front seat. I start pushing them out of the car and suddenly the bottle goes flying out of my hand and shatters against the curb. At the time, neither Farrah nor I think anything of it and hop out of the limo to take a cab to the theater. Another limo picks us up after the show, and on the way home, as we're telling the driver what happened earlier, he says that photographers pay limo drivers to say the car is stalled, that it's a standard trick. The whole thing was a setup. Soon after, a security guard from the Pierre who was supposed to have been protecting us that night claims I threw the bottle of Coke at him deliberately and injured his eye. He files a civil suit. The story is everywhere. The tabloids emphasized the fact that the security guard was a police officer (even though he was off duty at the time) and they turned the bottle, which never came into contact with anything except concrete, into my assault weapon. It becomes a ten-year battle costing me a hundred thousand dollars in legal fees. Farrah's testimony is persuasive and a jury ruled that the security guard was not entitled to any damages.

Yes, I could have settled, but for me this wasn't about money; it was about not getting taken. I end up having to sue my insurance agent because all my legal fees should have been covered by my homeowner's policy, but he never filed the claim. Welcome to the world of celebrity. Sadly, it will be only the first chapter of what will become a long, winding story of animosity between the press and me. I've been told I should have handled the media differently over the years. I never commented when asked if I had something to say because I didn't believe they'd quote me accurately. I thought I'd just be feeding the machine. A one-day story would turn into a week's worth of stories. And as my parents were fond of saying, "Today's headlines will line tomorrow's birdcages." Wisdom will come too late, but I didn't know that then.

It seems drama follows Farrah and me almost everywhere we go during that summer of 1982 in New York. One afternoon we're walking past the Russian Tea Room near Carnegie Hall, on Fifty-seventh Street, and a producer I know, Lester Persky, comes out of the restaurant, insisting that Farrah and I join him for tea. I'd met Lester through Andy Warhol and liked him. Several years later, he'll executive produce one of Farrah's most successful made-for-TV movies, *Poor Little Rich Girl*, about heiress Barbara Hutton. We agree to join him, and when we get to the table, the last person in the world I would want to see is sitting there: Diana Ross. We had a brief fling years earlier and unfortunately things did not end smoothly. The moment Diana spots us she bursts into tears and runs into the ladies' room. And she doesn't come out. Farrah is sympathetic and I don't have to explain. Farrah and I had had that conversation.

She'd asked around about me. She was neither shocked nor surprised that there had been beautiful women in my life before her and a few hearts were broken. "I never expected you to be celibate," Farrah said. "That would have shocked me. But I sure was relieved to learn you have a reputation for never cheating. I can't tell you who told me. She's a good friend of yours. She said not to worry. And I trust her." To this day, I don't know who my fairy godmother was.

Long before I met Farrah, Diana Ross and I were signed to costar in *The Bodyguard*. John Boorman, who made *Deliverance*, was the director. Diana was difficult and opinionated. All she did was complain about the script. We went through three screenplays. It would have been one thing if none of the scripts were good, but they were excellent. I eventually got fed up with her imperiousness and we never did do the picture. More than a decade later it would be made into a box office smash with Kevin Costner and Whitney Houston. And yes, Diana and I did have a brief fling during preproduction for the film. But she killed whatever spark there was between us when she put on her diva act. I remember taking her to the airport one day. I had a Rolls-Royce at the time, and we ran out of gas. I made her help me push the car to a gas station. I thought that was funny, this big star pushing a Rolls-Royce down Century Boulevard, cars whizzing past us. She didn't. I read her autobiography. I wasn't in it.

Farrah and I would travel back and forth to New York often in those early days. There are stirrings of trouble to come in our relationship, but like any couple in the grasp of romance, we ignore the clues. We make a special trip for Andy Warhol. I had met him several years earlier at a bar-restaurant popular with the downtown New York avant-garde crowd, Max's Kansas City, and to my surprise, we hit it off even though Andy was a man of few words, to say the least. I introduce Farrah to him at his legendary studio, the Factory. ABC's *20/20* is doing a story on him and they want to film him manufacturing a portrait of a pop star. Andy asks if I'd do him a favor and persuade Farrah to pose. I tell him I will if in turn, as a kind of payment, he gives me two copies of the portrait. He's happy to agree. One of those copies Farrah wills to the University of Texas, her alma mater. The other still hangs over my bed in Malibu. I'm currently in a dispute with the University of Texas over its ownership. We bring Tatum with us to Andy's studio, one of our many attempts to win her over. So we're at the Factory and Farrah's in this little dressing room area getting ready. All Andy needs from her is a series of Polaroids. She's taking forever so I open the door and she's upset at being interrupted. Righteous anger. Still, her response rubs me the wrong way. We're staying at the Pierre, and on the cab ride back I'm silent. I don't even go into the hotel with her and Tatum. I take a walk around the block to calm down. I didn't like being talked to as if I were a minion, especially when I'd organized the whole thing.

When I get to the hotel room, Farrah's drinking a bottle of soda, and suddenly I become convinced that she's going to hurl it right at my face. I knock it out of her hand. She's stunned. Her eyes well with tears. I storm out. Immediately afterward I feel terrible. Joanna used to do things like that, dangerous things. I had seen those weapons before. I was gun-shy. And so I overreacted, dramatically. Adding to my mortification, I ask Tatum to fix it for me, which surprisingly she does, smoothing things over with Farrah. I now realize just how severely being married to Joanna had affected me. Farrah also carried a lot of emotional baggage from her years with Lee Majors. We would both continue to be haunted by our marital histories.

Farrah's divorce is finalized in 1982, and as the weeks turn into months, we ease into the rhythms and routines of living together as a couple. She is living in the Antelo house. I sell my Beverly Hills home on the old John Barrymore estate to George Harrison's manager. And Farrah and I split our time between her house on Antelo and mine on Malibu Beach, with occasional romantic sojourns to my place in Big Sur, which I'll also sell several years later. Ted Turner will buy it. Whenever I see Jane Fonda, she always talks about how much she liked the Jacuzzi there. Farrah and I spent many wonderful nights in that Jacuzzi.

At this point, Tatum is living in her own apartment. I recognize now that at seventeen she was too young to have that degree of independence. It's one of my life's greatest regrets that I didn't establish stricter boundaries with my children. I was one of those fathers who placed too much value on being a friend to his kids and not enough on being a parent. How I wish someone had sat me down and warned me about the consequences of Malibu-style domesticity. Farrah would try but I could be one stubborn SOB, and all of us would pay the price.

The first deposit on that bill comes due in the new year. Griffin's behavior is growing more unpredictable and his demeanor more surly and secretive. He's also experimenting with drugs and alcohol, and I begin to fear the worst. Tatum will be next. She's always had a self-destructive rebellious streak, resenting any kind of authority or discipline from shoplifting laws to schoolteachers. During a brief stint in boarding school, she was nearly expelled for stealing jewelry from other students. She was eight. And her need for attention and affection is bottomless. It worries me. But at this point, she's distanced herself from Farrah and me, and my main concern is getting Griffin back on track. My other son, Patrick, thankfully seems to be doing okay. I have to give my second wife Leigh Taylor-Young credit. Though I may not understand her New Age philosophies and bohemian sensibilities, she's always been one hell of a mother, and it shows because of all my kids, Patrick is the one who was able to sidestep the temptations.

Though concerns about Griffin and Tatum are weighing heavily on Farrah and me, we also have careers that require constant attention, and if you take a breather in this industry, someone can knock you out of the game. As another Easter approaches, Farrah receives a call from the producers of *Extremities,* the hit off-Broadway play about a woman who turns the tables on her rapist. They're interested in having her replace Susan Sarandon. I take Farrah to New York, it's a rough play, a lot of work for an actress, and I notice that Susan is all banged up from the fight scenes. Farrah elbows me and says, "I can do this." So we return to Los Angeles and start preparing her for the role, learning the lines, practicing the dialogue, and blocking the scenes. We haven't made any commitment yet to the producers. I want to be sure she's ready. I know so much attention will be paid to Farrah that I don't want anything to go wrong, especially in New York, where the theater world can be uncompromising.

So picture this. I'm scrunched inside my fireplace in my bedroom in Malibu because Farrah and I are rehearsing that famous scene in which the rapist is trapped in the hearth. Farrah is deep in character. She's glowering at me and hurling obscenities, lost in the reality of the character she's portraying. Meanwhile the phone is ringing. Sue Mengers, who will soon be managing Farrah, keeps calling to tell me she can't keep the producers at bay much longer. I reach for the receiver, and I hear this huge grunt coming out of Farrah as she pulls a log out of the stack and lunges at me. I duck and press the phone to my ear. "She's ready," I tell Sue.

"Messenger the contracts." That was the thing about Farrah. She was fearless, hungry to take on the hardest roles. Beneath that big blond mane of hers was a steely will and courage to spare. She would come to need it in ways neither of us could have imagined on that afternoon of rough magic, me covered in soot, marveling at my girl, who was about to show everyone what she was made of.

While Farrah is in New York rehearsing for *Extremities*, I'm back in LA filming the comedy drama *Irreconcilable Differences* with Shelley Long and Drew Barrymore. Sharon Stone is in it too, one of her first movies. One day she asks me if I'll run off to Las Vegas and marry her. I tell her, "Can we do the honeymoon first?" I always liked Sharon. A graceful and determined woman, she was fun to work with. Director Charles Shyer was easy to work with too. He was nothing like Stanley Kubrick, whom I worked with on *Barry Lyndon*. Stanley's directorial method was to film a scene fifty times or more. He never explained why after, say, forty-one takes the next do over was needed. I once said to him after repeating a scene so many times I'd forgotten my name as well as my lines, "Stanley, you act my part in the scene. I'll watch and then imitate you." I was sincere. He thought I was trying to be funny and perceived it as insolence. My best guess is that he wanted to fatigue the actors and see what became of their performance when they were exhausted. In spite of being one of those worn-down actors, Stanley and I shared a mutual respect.

Stanley was less extravagant as a producer. He would continually review the schedule and the budget for *Barry Lyndon*, the two documents that Stanley the director often ignored. But in his role as producer, Stanley was acutely aware of costs. He'd count the rolls of toilet paper and ration them; only so many would be available per day.

During the production of *Irreconcilable Differences*, I was staying at Farrah's house on Antelo. I come home one night and see Griffin pulling out of the garage, his car loaded with Farrah's belongings, end tables, antique lamps, knick-knacks. He can't even see out the back window. I run up to the driver's side and yank open the door. "What the hell are you doing?" I say. "Put it all back!" He makes a smart-ass remark and then gets out of the car. He's violent and irrational. He's got this empty look in his eyes. I can feel years of resentment radiating off his skin. He swings at me. I block. Then he dives and knocks both my feet out from under me. I hit the pavement elbows first. I get up. He comes at me again, this time following me into the house. We fight and knock over the curio cabinet. I fall into the broken glass, cutting my elbows and knees. "What are you doing," I keep yelling at him. "Stop!" Some nineteen-year-old sons think they can take their dads, and he wasn't going to stop until he did. He again goes for my legs, this time tripping me. I don't remember hitting him in the mouth. But by then, my survival instinct had taken over.

Twenty minutes later we're on our hands and knees together, searching for his lost teeth. That night, I hold my child in my arms while he sleeps, wondering how this once sweet boy, who comforted me when I gave up the lead in *The Champ* because he hadn't been cast as the son, could be the same young man who hours before was primed to maim me.

I call Farrah to let her know what happened. I hated dragging her into my messes with my kids. But she had become the person whose judgment I relied on most, the only one who could give me a sense of balance when chaos was threatening to spill over me. She doesn't complain about the damage to the interior of her beautiful home. She just listens with compassion and understanding. A little less than two years later, after our son Redmond is born, I'm sure she must have recalled that conversation—me out of my mind with anger and sadness, she, exhausted from rehearsals, desperately trying to calm me—and wondered, *What have I brought this innocent new life into?*

The next morning I have to go back to work. I must shoot a scene shirtless that day, and in the film, if you look closely enough, you can see the evidence of the previous night's brawl on my arms, which are decorated with cuts and bruises. Making matters worse, while I'm on set, Griffin calls his mother. She picks him up and brings him straight to a photographer. She sells the story to *People,* and the celebrity magazines feast. Soon after, I send Griffin to Habilitate for rehab. He'll stay for a year.

During that time, *People* will run another piece, this

time a feature on Griffin, and to my surprise, their coverage of me is okay. Early in my career, the press treated me fairly. I got good reviews for good performances, poor reviews for poor performances, and press interest in the women I dated was more respectful than salacious. It was my lack of parenting skills that inspired their ire.

Whenever *Irreconcilable Differences* runs on cable I'm reminded of this shameful episode with my child. The debacle will further sour my relationship with Tatum, who thinks I've turned my back on her brother by sending him to Habilitate. I can't make her understand that the opposite is true. This is one of the foremost drug rehabilitation facilities in the Western world, and besides, it's located in idyllic Hawaii.

When Farrah opens in *Extremities,* I can't be there because I'm still shooting *Irreconcilable Differences.* Though it couldn't be helped, it still bothers me that I wasn't by her side opening night. And what an opening night it was! When I telephone Farrah, she says that a man in the audience, who we later discover had been stalking her, rushed the stage, angry that she'd never signed his poster. "What did you do?" I ask. "They dragged him away and we started the scene over." She's telling me all this as if it were just a glitch. I'm amazed by this girl. Most actresses I know would have been rattled by something like that. There would come a time in her life when that sanguinity would abandon her, but that's all in the future. Now she's still the Farrah I fell in love with, the one I've never stopped loving. After the scare with the crazy fan, the producers hire two security guards, one for each side of the stage, to make sure nothing like that happens again. It's a clockwork production from that night on. Farrah receives rave reviews and packs the house every performance. She is an actress now.

Once I wrap on *Irreconcilable Differences*, I hurry to New York to stay with Farrah. She's at her most radiant, soaking up the long overdue respect from an industry that had once considered her only that blonde in the bathing suit from *Charlie's Angels*. It's wonderful to be spending time in New York together. Though we're not night owls, every once in a while we'll go dancing at Studio 54. We went there out of curiosity. Bianca Jagger had her birthday bash there in '77 or '78. I knew the building. It's where Johnny Carson's show was broadcast. Steve Rubell and Ian Schrager converted it from a theater. The space was huge. I used to think that if Farrah wandered away, it could take all weekend to find her. We always danced. Farrah could float across the floor. I should have let her lead. There were a number of songs we claimed as our own and always got up to move to them. More than thirty years later I can still remember the words to Donna Summer's "Last Dance." Farrah and I also spent a lot of time in the balcony, where there were tables and a great view. Above the balcony was terra incognita. The third floor housed the infamous rubber room, so named because it could be hosed down after all the open sex and drugs. I was intrigued. Farrah had less than no interest so we never went up there. Not quite never. I peeked once: it was like something out of a Brueghel painting. We never had to use the main entrance. There was a VIP door around the back where we'd invariably meet people we knew: Andy and Liza, Michael Jackson and Liz Taylor. I think Salvador Dalí was there one night with someone who strongly resembled Elton John. When owner Steve Rubell is charged with tax evasion, most of his friends desert him. Farrah and I take him out to a very public dinner.

Though Farrah's schedule is demanding, when she does get time off, we sometimes go to Montauk, the most distant Hampton, and stay with Andy Warhol. Farrah loves the beach and the sun. I enjoy Andy, as odd as he sometimes is. He acts as if he adores Farrah so they get on famously. And she loves art. Andy's place has five classic clapboard houses designed by Stanford White. He bought it in partnership with Paul Morrissey, director of many of Andy's early avant-garde firms. (They paid $225,000; the compound was recently on sale for $50 million.) The Rolling Stones took breaks from their tours and rehearsed their albums there in the seventies. It was comfortable and refreshing, with an astonishing view of the sand dunes and the ocean, and the company was never less than invigorating. Bianca Jagger without Mick, Yves Saint Laurent opening clams in the kitchen, the fashion designer Halston dishing the divas, and, of course, the neighbors: Edward Albee, Bobby De Niro, and Paul Simon. For reasons I never understood, Dick Cavett insisted on playing Frisbee sans clothing. Maybe he was working up an appetite.

It was there I learned that even the famous can be impressed by the somewhat more famous, as certain people never ceased mentioning that they were there that memorable weekend Liz or Liza or John Lennon visited. The first time we go we encounter Bianca. Farrah never warms up to her. She ran with a more cultured, artistic group than we knew in LA. Farrah felt threatened by her, though she had no reason to be and my behavior was as proper as an English butler's. Maybe it was because Bianca was always topless, and Farrah knew she and I were once lovers. Bianca and I remained friends and I still think of her that way even though we haven't spoken in ten years.

Later that year Farrah does another made-for-TV movie, *The Red-Light Sting,* in San Francisco with Beau Bridges. I visit her on set and even manage to squeeze in a quick trip to see my son Patrick, who's living in Carmel and attending the Stevenson School. *The Red-Light Sting* is a fourteen-day shoot for which Farrah has an A-list payday. Though the movie itself is forgettable, it's important to her in that she's finally starting to know what it feels like to have money and a career without someone taking a cut. The three decades Farrah and I are together; I honor her need to remain in control of her own finances. We maintain separate bank accounts, and of course I'm traditional in that I pay

for whatever she'll allow me to—dinner, travel, presents—
but when it comes to her income, I respect her privacy and
her independence. Though Farrah and I would argue about
a lot during the turbulent years of our relationship, one subject we rarely had words over was money. It is said that sta-
tistically the two biggest issues that destroy marriages are
money and kids. Perhaps God gave us a break on the former
because he knew the latter would be so sad.

The 1983 holidays are a welcome respite, though I miss
Tatum and continue to worry about Griffin. Farrah and I fly
to Hawaii to see him at Habilitate, and while he seems to be
trying hard to turn his life around, it's as if he's been severed
from his own soul, and like the headless horseman, he's trying to find the top of him and put it back on.

I immerse myself in loving my girl and working with her
to further develop her craft. Inspiration strikes from a surprising source. Farrah has a subscription to *Texas Monthly*.
One morning over coffee, I'm scanning the latest issue and
there's a piece on Candy Barr, the famous stripper who had
an affair with the notorious Mickey Cohen and performed
in Jack Ruby's Dallas nightclub. She shot her second husband, a crime for which she served three years in prison.
I'd always been intrigued by her story. A star in burlesque,
when she was sixteen years old, she appeared in the most
famous stag film of all time, *Smart Alec,* aka *Smart Aleck*.
It's a memorable performance for those of us men who saw
it in our youth. It ranks right up there with Rita Hayworth

in *Gilda*. Years later, history would remember Candy Barr as an unlikely feminist. I point out the article to Farrah and suggest that this would be a perfect vehicle for her. There are some striking similarities between the two of them, both having had to overcome implacable misconceptions. Farrah's excited by the idea and we go to San Antonio to meet Candy. She's a tougher broad than I thought she would be and Farrah is fascinated by her. In fact, when we return home, Farrah insists that we watch *Smart Alec* together. She's never asked to watch a porn movie before and I must admit I'm excited. We were both self-conscious for the entire eleven minutes but not embarrassed. And I can tell you that Candy Barr had nothing on Farrah. We were still glowing when we woke up the next morning.

We enter into a development deal with Atlantic Pictures. We already have one enthusiastic investor who once saw Farrah dance and thinks she would be perfect for the burlesque scenes. It's my first time playing producer and I want to get it right, so I hire George Axelrod to write the script. He'd written *Bus Stop* and *The Seven Year Itch* for Marilyn Monroe, *Breakfast at Tiffany's* with Audrey Hepburn, *The Manchurian Candidate;* his credits read like a graduate course at the USC film school. Unfortunately, George and I disagree vehemently on the screenplay. I want to tell the story of Candy Barr as a young woman, and he insists on writing the story of her as an old woman. The project is stillborn. The experience gives me new appreciation

for the responsibilities and challenges of being a producer.
Putting all those elements together ain't easy. Could it have
been a great start vehicle for Farrah? Might it have begun a
new career for me as a producer/director?

S pring 1984 arrives, and with it big news. Farrah is pregnant. I'm surprised and delighted. Though I know she
had always wanted children, it's not something we ever discussed. While I'm overjoyed, she's veiled, ambiguous. My
problems with Griffin and Tatum have taken their toll. She's
afraid to bring another O'Neal into the world. That fear has
been simmering for years and we've avoided talking about it.
We avoid it again now. As the months pass, the slow expan-
sion of her belly will ease her fears. But that first trimester
will prove challenging.

CHAPTER THREE

AND BABY MAKES
THREE

The pregnancy proves more difficult than we anticipate. Morning sickness saps Farrah's energy. I spend many hours holding her head over the toilet. Farrah and I attend birthing classes together, a new experience for me. I'm the modern father-to-be, rubbing cream on my girl's tummy, massaging her calves, and tending to her needs. I've been an expectant father before, but I never loved Joanna or Leigh the same way I love Farrah. The traditionalist in me says that Farrah and I should make things legal now, but with three failed marriages between us, there's another part that says why change something that's working? After the baby is born, Farrah will ask me to marry her. I'll foolishly sidestep the question and she won't press me.

After Redmond's birth, she begins the made-for-TV movie *The Burning Bed*. It's based on the true story of a battered wife who after being brutally raped by her husband kills him in his sleep by setting the bed on fire. Though her recent run off-Broadway with *Extremities* was a success, theater doesn't have the same reach as television. All during the production of *The Burning Bed* I could feel it. This would be the one. I watch Farrah abandon herself to

the role. There's a courtroom scene in which her character is on the witness stand describing how her husband let
her puppy freeze to death. Farrah is crying and mucous is
running from her nose. This is Farrah Fawcett at her best,
her considerable skills fully realized. Her risky performance
will astound both the public and the industry. Reviewers
will comment that they'd never seen anybody that disheveled look so beautiful. *The Burning Bed* is huge. It isn't just a
successful movie. It makes the editorial pages for revealing a
dirty secret in America: the judges and the lawyers, the po-
licemen and the politicians, the doctors and the investment
bankers, the men considered part of society's elite who beat
their wives and then get away with it, hiding behind their
badges and their gavels and their thousand-dollar suits. *The
Burning Bed* exposes them. It sparks new legislation against
domestic violence and becomes part of the women's rights
agenda. And when it airs, the ratings are historic. The network's publicity department sends Farrah thick binders full
of scrapbook-worthy reviews. Farrah is asked to speak on
behalf of battered women and does a series of interviews and
events in support of the anti–domestic violence movement.

Farrah is nominated for an Emmy, but she doesn't win.
She didn't expect to win so she didn't prepare a speech. Her
satisfaction has come from knowing she played the part well.
Farrah doesn't need public affirmation the way I do. Joanne
Woodward gets the Emmy that year for *Do You Remember
Love,* portraying a professor suffering from Alzheimer's. In

truth, Farrah's performance was more nuanced. I remember sitting with Farrah that night at the awards ceremony, squeezing her hand, both of us listening to the list of nominees being called. I was so sure she'd win. When they announce Joanne Woodward's name, it's a kick in the chest. She's not even there to accept. "Let's go, honey," I tell her. "I've got to get out of this place." I start to rise, and Farrah gently touches my forearm and gives me this wan smile. "No, that wouldn't be fair to Joanne," she whispers. It's always bothered me when the media depicted Farrah as unsophisticated. They couldn't have been more wrong. Farrah is also nominated for a Golden Globe for *The Burning Bed*, but you know who wins one? Paul Le Mat, who played the part of the guy who beats her. He wins while she carries the movie, although Paul is excellent.

That night we skipped the Emmy parties and drove back to Malibu. We took a bottle of Cristal Rose with us down to the beach, sat on the sand, and watched the moon rise over Catalina Island, and for once thought about how fortunate we were.

On the family front, the situation with Tatum is tentative at best. She reminds me of a jungle cat, graceful, commanding, and yet always wary. She started dating tennis bad boy John McEnroe a couple of years before. It will not be a match made in heaven. She managed to steer clear of addiction all those years living with her mother and brother, not to mention having a father who didn't always set the best example where drugs and alcohol were concerned, and then she falls for a famous athlete who you'd think would be squeaky clean, and instead they do drugs together.

Farrah and I meet John for the first time when Tatum brings him for a visit to the beach house. There I am sitting in the living room, looking at him and thinking to myself, *Dear God, he's thin. He's the number one tennis player?* He's watching my face and he's perceptive. He lifts his left wrist, twists it, and says, "It's all in here." Like everyone else, I knew his reputation for arrogant bursts of adrenaline both on and off the court, but seeing him with my daughter, her face beaming with adoration, his arm wrapped protectively around her shoulders, I'm relieved that my baby's finally found someone. *Maybe*, I tell myself hopefully, *he'll settle her.* I was wrong.

As the birth of our child nears, Farrah and I are buoyant about the future. Patrick is delighted. Grif wonders aloud, "Why do you want one more of us?" And from Tatum we receive overly polite congratulations.

Our commitment deepens. That isn't to say it's perfect. When you live with someone, eventually that person will see the unvarnished you. I know that Farrah is never on time, but I'm one of those guys who likes to get there early, and early for Farrah means only being an hour late. It drives me nuts, but I'm able to restrain my annoyance. I'm also finding out that she can become cranky if she doesn't get her sleep, and can that woman sleep! I'm always up and dressed before she's even begun to stir. At the time, I wax romantic about having my very own Sleeping Beauty.

While I'm learning to accept her idiosyncrasies, she, too, is becoming familiar with mine. *Irreconcilable Differences* opens and doesn't meet box office expectations. The reviews are mixed and while some actors may feign nonchalance when it comes to the critics, we're all too human, and when someone whose opinion carries weight has less than flattering things to say about your work, it can hurt.

JOURNAL ENTRY, SEPTEMBER 24, 1984
We've opened lukewarm. I stop for the trades, *Variety* and the *Hollywood Reporter,* to read their box office numbers. I got so disgusted that I went to Dutton's on San Vicente to get my mind off my most recent box office flop. I bought the new Le Carré and a bio of Teddy Roosevelt by Edmund Morris that was recommended by Doug Dutton. I also picked up a copy of *The Leopard,* an Italian novel made into a movie by Luchino Visconti, starring one of my idols, Burt Lancaster. When I get home, Farrah's talking on the phone with her press agent and can't be bothered. I pace back and forth until she finally pays attention to me.

Reading through my journals, I wince at some of my childish behavior. I'm aware of these extreme ups and downs in my life. One day I love someone to death; the next I'm wishing that person were never born. This emotional immaturity explains why I've always struggled with close relationships. And it was no exception with Farrah. Sometimes she would humor me during an outburst. Other times she'd chastise me. More often she'd just laugh. If I was having a meltdown, she'd watch me storm out of the room without saying a word because she knew in twenty minutes I'd come back in fine spirits. We learned the ebbs and flows of each other's moods and became adept at intuiting what was needed to get through a rough patch.

Later that fall, I begin shooting *Fever Pitch* on location in Las Vegas with Catherine Hicks and Giancarlo Giannini. It's being directed by Richard Brooks, who made *Cat on a Hot Tin Roof*, *In Cold Blood*, *Elmer Gantry*, *Looking for Mr. Goodbar*. Brooks is old school and known to brandish his walking cane when an actor doesn't hit his mark. Actors don't appreciate a compliment from Richard Brooks, an irascible genius; they covet it. I like listening to his stories, especially about Humphrey Bogart. Brooks wrote the screenplay for *Key Largo*, which John Huston directed. I knew John Huston. His daughter Anjelica was one of the great dalliances of my postadolescence. And my adolescence lasted longer than most. Marriage and parenthood may have ended my childhood, but nothing has ever interrupted my adolescence. So Brooks tells me how one day he's having lunch with Bogart. This is when Bogart is in the advance stages of esophageal cancer. Most of his stomach has been removed. Remember, Bogart was a smoker. Almost every scene he's in, you see a cigarette dangling from his lips, and when he does get cancer, it will ravage him quickly. So they're eating and Brooks says he can hear the faint thud of food dropping into Bogart's lower abdomen. Now Brooks is an ex-marine who'd fought on Guam and Guadalcanal, places few survived. Bogart looks at him and says, "Can't you take it, kid?"

Brooks's reverence for Bogart is apparent. He tells me about the time he, Bogie, and Bacall were in the limo en route to the Academy Awards. Bogie had been nominated for Best Actor for *The African Queen*, which he made with Katharine Hepburn. Brooks asks him if he's prepared something to say, just in case. Bogie laughs, saying that he hasn't because he'll never win. Brooks hastily scribbles comments on a piece of paper for him, which Bogie doesn't take, insisting he won't need it. So Bacall takes the note, and when Bogart's name is announced as the winner and he stands, she slips it into his tuxedo pocket and says, "Read this." Of course he doesn't, and he stumbles through his overlong acceptance speech. Brooks says it's the only time he ever saw the great Humphrey Bogart flub. "But that was Bogie," Brooks says. "He was humble. He really didn't think he had a chance."

There's a lot of buzz about *Fever Pitch*. I begin to feel

optimistic again about my career, hopeful that this will be my comeback vehicle. And like any man, when things are going well at work, the benefits are also manifest at home, especially in the bedroom.

But back to *Fever Pitch*. I enjoy working with Brooks, though I don't always like the way he treats his crew. It can become easy for actors and directors to take for granted the valuable contributions of these men and women to the movie-making process, and I've always tried to give crew members the respect they deserve. When the fine actor Christian Bale went off on a rant recently against one of the crew during the shoot for *Terminator,* and it went viral over the Internet, for once I was grateful to TMZ and Radar Online for giving Bale, and every other actor who was shocked by all the adverse media coverage, a lesson in humility.

I've had more than my share of those, one of which will come with the release of *Fever Pitch*. It will make my disappointment over *Irreconcilable Differences* seem silly by comparison. Though I don't know it then, Brooks's final film will earn less than six hundred thousand dollars and be nominated for four Razzie Awards, including Worst Picture. The Razzies, which are handed out the same week as the Oscars, are meant to be in good fun, an example of Hollywood's winking at itself, and at the time, I, too, laugh it off, thinking, *Well, at least we're in good company.* Stallone sweeps the Razzies with *First Blood II* and *Rocky IV.* Over the next several years, these disappointments will have a corrosive effect on Farrah and me.

JOURNAL ENTRY, OCTOBER 10, 1984
The baby just kicked for the first time. I massage my darling's shoulders until she falls asleep.

Farrah visits me on location for *Fever Pitch* in Las Vegas. She's just been featured on the covers of *People* and *Us* magazines for *The Burning Bed*. Farrah is so fit that except for her tiny baby bump, which she can easily camouflage, you'd never know she was six months pregnant. During the photo shoot for *People*, she doesn't say anything about being pregnant. They find out after the issue hits the stands and are furious. Eager to take advantage of their competitor's oversight, *Us* immediately runs another cover story on Farrah; only this one is about the pregnancy. I'm bemused by it all. Farrah and I are getting used to this roller-coaster ride with the press. Sometimes we feel like hostages at an amusement park.

Tatum slides in for a visit. The princess of diminishing has returned. I get the feeling that my daughter will never trust men. One moment she's sitting with Farrah discussing baby names; the next she's telling Farrah that I'm going to throw her away when I grow tired of her, the same way I did all the other women in my life. Farrah considers the source and isn't worried, but I am. With Farrah pregnant, the last thing I want is a confrontation between these two. While they never actually fight, on set I'm distracted, concerned about them spending time together. I thought Tatum's first serious relationship would change all that. I know now her wounds were much deeper and more complex than any of us understood. But back then she didn't seem moodier than any postadolescent woman in love with a bad boy. Little did I know that John McEnroe would aggravate those wounds.

Fever Pitch wraps the week after Thanksgiving. Upon our return to LA, Barbara Walters interviews Farrah for one of her ABC evening specials. She's in her ninth month and positively radiant on camera. I'm often asked why Barbara didn't interview Farrah and me as a couple. I suspect the idea made the network queasy with Farrah so obviously pregnant and our not being married. Today I see news stories about expectant celebrity couples, and no one seems to care about their marital status. Maybe they should. Farrah and I were lucky. We were never overtly criticized for having a child without benefit of clergy. We never hired a publicist to handle the story of her pregnancy. We just lived our lives. It didn't seem to affect our careers.

Farrah and I spend the holidays in Malibu. As I was going through my journals for this book, I found an entry from that New Year's morning that gave me pause. Tatum and John had come to LA to attend a party. They brought Patrick to the party with them. They all stayed at the beach house with Farrah and me.

JOURNAL ENTRY, JANUARY 1, 1985
John and Tate have left for the airport to fly to Las Vegas so he can play tomorrow against Conners. Tatum's first match. After they left, Patrick told me something unusual. When they got home last night at four a.m., Tatum wanted to continue to party, which included tequila shots and pool until sunrise. Poor Patrick finally put her to bed after she started to see the pool balls two at a time.

I was so relieved to see Tatum and Farrah getting along for a change that I didn't worry that my daughter, who'd never been a drinker, who would confiscate my glass when she was a little girl, had gotten wasted the night before. Farrah had admitted to me two months earlier, when she was seven months pregnant, that Tatum and John had offered her cocaine. I was surprised because at the time Tatum was still proclaiming her objections to drugs and alcohol. I assumed John was the instigator and Tatum just went along.

The more things devolved with Tatum, the more determined I was to get it right with the new baby. What I didn't understand back then is that every day you're a parent is another chance to make things right, no matter how old your children are. That's why I'm still trying with Tatum even as I write this.

But back to January of 1985. Our first trip to the hospital is a false alarm. I still chuckle about what happens next.

We return home and the moment we walk in the door, Farrah asks me for her special blanket. I have no idea what she means. I'd never heard her mention any blanket before, so I skip to the linen closet and grab the first one I see. "No, that's not it," she says. "I want my blankie, get me my *blankie!*" She's near tears and I still haven't a clue what she is talking about. I say, "Farrah, I don't know which one that is, you've never asked me for a blankie before." She replies, "The one in the bag!" She must be referring to the suitcase we'd packed for the hospital, so I lope to the garage to retrieve it. Pleased with my quick thinking, I hand it to her. "No, that's not it either!" she cries. Suddenly I see a cab pulling into the driveway and Farrah's mom, Pauline, getting out. Relief washes over me. The Mounties in the form of my unfriendly mother-in-law have come to the rescue. Momma soon retrieves her daughter's sacred bit of burgundy cloth.

The next trip isn't a false alarm. Farrah is determined to have an all-natural birth: no drugs and no epidural. We'd decided on the alternative birth center at Valley Presbyterian. Farrah's room looks more like a deluxe suite at the Four Seasons than a hospital room. They hook her up to a machine to monitor her contractions. This is all brand-new to me. I wasn't present for the births of my other children. Back then, fathers were banished to the waiting room.

An hour goes by; nothing's happening and Farrah starts to get bored. "Let's take a walk around the maternity ward and see who else is here," she says. "With all those wires?"

I ask. Next thing I know, Farrah is out of bed and on her feet, tiptoeing down the hall, peeking into the other rooms, waving hello to people, while I'm behind her pushing the monitor. The dial starts to beep and it's getting louder. "Honey, don't you think we should go back?" I say. Just then she's hit with her first big labor pain. "Please, for the love of God, can we go back now, Farrah?" So we turn around like a little choo-choo and head to our suite.

Now she's in full labor, and she's pushing, pushing. Hours go by. Something's wrong. All we can see is the crown of the baby's head. The doctors ask me to leave the room. When I'm finally called back in, a drenched, exhausted Farrah grabs my hand and squeezes it; then she gives one final brave push. Our son enters the world on January 30, 1985. I'm elated. He's blond except for a bright red shock of hair at the nape of his neck. We decide to call him Redmond, which was also the name of the character I played in *Barry Lyndon*.

Motherhood completes Farrah. All of her natural maternal instincts are on display. She's attentive and calm. Farrah and Redmond are inseparable. We spend happy, lazy days with our new baby, relishing every early milestone, the first smile and the first crawl. We cocoon ourselves that spring and summer, somehow both of us knowing we may never again experience such simple joy in our lives.

Autumn brings new challenges and opportunities. Griffin leaves Habilitate vowing to stay clean, and Tatum will soon be pregnant with her second child. She and John buy Johnny Carson's house down the beach from me. And Farrah is about to start shooting the film version of *Extremities*. I'm holding down the domestic front and reviewing scripts in search of my next film project. I'm eager to get back to work, and though I miss acting, being a stay-at-home dad fulfills me. Feeding and changing Redmond, rocking him to sleep, bathing him, listening to his musical cooing, all remind me of my sweetest memories of Tatum. When she was an infant, we shared a private world. I couldn't get her to fall asleep one night and I'd tried everything, so out of desperation, I placed her on the dryer after I'd just put in a load, hoping the warmth of the machine would lull her to sleep. Within moments she was comatose. It worked every time. Being with Redmond conjures up all those teary images. On one level, it gives me something hopeful to cling to during this long estrangement from my daughter, but it also makes me yearn even more for what we once had. And Tatum continues to be unpredictable. One day she's effusive and warm, coming over to visit Farrah and me, offering to babysit her little brother; and two days later she'll be distant and stormy, refusing to return our phone calls. I suspect some of it may be at John's request. I can only imagine what Tatum has said, and if I were he, and the mother of my unborn child had been telling me what a bastard her dad had been all her life, I'd be inclined to put distance between my family and the father too.

Tatum and John make an effort to include Patrick in their life, and gradually he begins pulling away from me. Not anything overt, just a subtle, quiet shift in his affection. I can't blame him, but I miss his staying with me when he has a free weekend. Patrick has always loved sports, and John, whom Patrick idolizes, is generous with him, taking him to tournaments and celebrity events, treating him like a younger brother. I pass John and Tatum's house on my daily beach run. If Patrick's there, he'll occasionally join me for a mile or two, but I can sense he's uncomfortable, as if he's being disloyal to Tatum. He shouldn't have to choose between his dad and sister any more than I should have to choose between the woman I love and my only daughter. What makes this tawdry tug-of-war even sadder is that I don't think Tatum is aware of what she's doing to her family. It's a debilitating survival instinct and it makes my heart ache for her. Sometimes when I'm passing the house, the curtains are drawn, but I see Tatum's silhouette in the window, watching. She doesn't invite me in or even wave hello. I tell myself it's okay, that in time things will get better for all of us. On those afternoons when I return from my run, Farrah will ask what's wrong. Too often I'll snap at her, not wanting to explain because I'm embarrassed. She'll gently coax the truth out, then keep trying to reassure me that this is an adjustment period for everyone and that I must be patient. I wish I could believe it was that simple.

The rest of the year goes quickly. *Extremities* wraps

without a hitch. When Farrah was shooting the made-for-TV movie *Nazi Hunter: The Beate Klarsfeld Story* on location in Paris, Christmas was doubly busy as we readied for the trip, mommy, baby, and me. Redmond's first birthday is punctuated by a series of routine inoculations required to take him out of the country. Farrah and I expect the poor little guy to wail all the way through. As we're filling out the forms at the pediatrician's, we almost reconsider. When the doctor walks in, Redmond gives him this big toothless smile and coos. I see Farrah welling up. I grab her hand. The doctor starts filling the syringe. Farrah and I hold our breath. He inserts the needle. Redmond lets out a big, defiant howl, and then he's fine. Days later we're on our way to the City of Lights.

These television productions are not glamorous. Farrah is on the set twelve to fourteen hours a day, often having to go through multiple wardrobe, hair, and makeup changes. It's physically exhausting, and though she holds up under the pressure, it's as if she's being tipped over every day and emptied. And it's not easy for her being away from Redmond. Her dilemma isn't unlike that of every working mother. Her only free time is late in the evening, and by then she's depleted and the baby's fast asleep. Often, she'll have to memorize lines for a scene the next morning before she can turn in. Some nights, she's too tired to eat, and I'll sit next to her in bed with Redmond cuddled between us, and rub her feet, reassuring her that soon we'll be home.

We brought a nanny with us, which allows me the

freedom to spend a few hours on set each day. I'll usually have the nanny bring Redmond by late in the afternoon, so that Farrah can see him while he's awake. Farrah's a trouper. She never complains, but when Redmond and I are leaving, her bright eyes go dull. Though I'm the one able to enjoy Paris with Redmond, watching her practice her craft with such abandon, despite the difficult circumstances, is making me wish the situation were reversed. It's hard on both of us. We pretend it's just temporary. If we'd talked out our feelings, resentments might not have accumulated. At times I feel impotent. Great roles, such as Michael Caine's in *Hannah and Her Sisters,* parts I was ready for, were passing me by. I'd become James Mason to Farrah's Judy Garland: it wasn't my star aborning. I stopped reading the trades and the *International Herald Tribune.* Once I was an insider. Now I'm a mere observer. I've become a bouillabaisse of steaming feelings. As much as I detested the paparazzi, the day they lowered their cameras when they saw me alone forced me to realize that whatever magic I'd once had was gone.

Paris, as someone once said, is a movable feast. We're staying at the Elysées Parc Monceau, a historic hotel near the Arc de Triomphe. The night we arrive we're too wide-awake from the flight to sleep, so at 2 a.m. Farrah and I, with Redmond tucked cozily in his pram, stroll down the Champs-Elysées. It remains a favorite memory and one of the few times Farrah and I are able to walk the streets of Paris without being accosted by photographers or fans.

In the mid-eighties the paparazzi were an even bigger challenge in France than in the States. There are nights when if we want to venture outside of our hotel for dinner, we must wait until after midnight for the photographers to disband. I try to keep Farrah's spirits up by making her laugh. Redmond is more of a natural at it than I, with his curly red hair and pudgy, curious little fingers, always reaching for something new to examine. And this shoot is Farrah's toughest yet. She portrays a German housewife who, with the help of her Jewish husband, launches a campaign to bring Nazi war criminals to justice after World War II. Farrah has to learn how to speak with a German accent, and it doesn't come easily, requiring hours of practice on top of her already demanding schedule.

And while I take care of her and Redmond the best I can, my frustrations are on the rise. Though I tell myself that this is Farrah's moment and I'm here for her and our baby, I can't pretend my dwindling career hasn't affected me. There's a possible role for me in a movie about professional bicycle racing. I agree to do it, and then just as I start to look forward to the project, the deal comes apart. The film is never made.

Meanwhile, Farrah's mood isn't bright either. When you're an actor and have internalized the character, by the end of filming it's sometimes difficult to know where the character ends and you begin again. Many actors choose to live in character the duration of a production, and while I admire their dedication to their craft, I've always believed it's one of the reasons why the divorce rate among serious actors is so high. Imagine being married to the ruthless villain or the wily seductress. I'm familiar with what some of these spouses have to endure while their husband or wife is deep into a role. And what if you're both actors? The more I think about it, the more I realize that Farrah and I are beating the odds.

Though I hate to leave Farrah and Redmond, Tatum is due around Mother's Day and she's extended me an olive branch. She wants me there for the birth of my first grandchild. Farrah cries when I leave, but I know I'm doing the right thing, and I tell myself I'll be gone for only a few days.

When I'm on the plane and the fasten-seatbelt light goes off, I take my favorite book of the moment out of my carry-on, *A Confederacy of Dunces.* I open it to where I had finished reading last night and discover that what I thought was my bookmark is actually a folded sheet, a letter Farrah must have written and slipped in this morning before I left, knowing I wouldn't begin to read it until after my flight had departed. I open it.

MY DARLING,

I already miss you terribly. And don't be mad at me, but knowing you're a thousand miles away at thirty thousand feet in the sky makes it easier to tell you what I need to say. Ryan, I'm scared. I know

your career isn't where you want it to be right now,
but you and I both know that's only temporary
and will change. Though you've been wonderful
to me in Paris and terrific with Redmond, please
tell me I shouldn't be afraid of losing you because
of my career. My life with you and our son is more
important to me than any TV movie. I'd walk away
from all of that if it would put the light back in your
eyes. I think this trip to see Tatum will be good for
you both. Please call me as soon as you arrive and
tell me you're safe. I love you with all my heart.

FARRAH

I call Farrah from the airport in Los Angeles and tell her not to be afraid, that I'm proud of her success and with her help, I'm sure I can get out of this funk I've been in. When I arrive at the hospital in Los Angeles, my daughter is glowing. On May 23, 1986, she makes me the proud grandfather of a baby boy, Kevin McEnroe. Four days later, Tatum and the baby are back home in Malibu and I'm visiting with them. John has returned to New York to get the house ready. She and the baby will be joining him soon. The phone rings. Tatum answers and I watch her face turn ashen. "Dad, there's been a terrible accident."

CHAPTER FOUR

FEVER PITCH

Tatum puts her hand over the mouthpiece and repeats to me what she's hearing. "They were in a boat on the Chesapeake Bay. Griffin cut between two slow-moving boats. He didn't know that one boat was towing the other. He saw the rope at the last second and ducked. Gio was practically decapitated."

It's beyond my worst fear.

Griffin was on location in Maryland working with director Francis Ford Coppola on the Viet Nam picture *Gardens of Stone*. He was starring in the film and Coppola's son Gian-Carlo was on the crew. Francis had worked with Griffin on *The Escape Artist* several years earlier and liked him. He knew Griffin was having a rough time and wanted to help him restart.

Gian-Carlo Coppola was twenty-two when he died, a year older than Griffin. At first Griffin denied that he was driving the boat and tried to place the blame on Gian-Carlo. The truth eventually came out. I imagine the scene over and over. He's had a few too many, he's feeling invincible. He spots these two slow-moving craft up ahead, and can't resist. He guns the engine. Thinks he'll have some fun. Adding to the tragedy, Gian-Carlo's fiancée was two months pregnant. She would bear him a son whom he would never know. After a short trial, Griffin will be charged with reckless boating, fined two hundred dollars, and sentenced to eighteen months probation. They won't be able to convict him of a felony because police never tested his blood for alcohol. Sometime after the trial, Gian-Carlo's mother, Eleanor, calls me. I never saw her in the courtroom. She expresses sympathy for what I'm going through with Griffin, and suggests he might benefit from therapy. Here's a woman who just lost her son, and she's consoling the father of the person responsible for his death, offering support. It takes me a moment to find my voice. "I wish it had been me and not your son," I tell her. "I mean that." And I did. Griffin never worked in the movie business again. To my surprise, Francis replaced Griffin and Gian-Carlo and continued filming.

But that's all later. I'm still listening to Tatum relaying the details of the accident and my mind is racing. I've also got Farrah and Redmond in Paris waiting for me, and the night before when I talked to her, Farrah didn't sound good. "And you're absolutely sure your brother wasn't driving?" I ask Tatum. "Dad, he's saying no, and I believe him." A part of me knows it had to have been my son behind that wheel. Griffin feeds on danger. But like Tatum, I was desperate to believe he was telling the truth. I was also concerned about Farrah, alone in Paris. Despite her protests, I could tell by the tone of her voice that she wanted me there.

So after doing what I can for Griffin, I leave for Paris on the Concorde. I bring along Patrick, who's on summer break. The tabloids are feasting on the story about Gian-Carlo's death and I want to protect Patrick, who's already been approached by reporters hoping he'll give them some headline quote about his brother. Though I knew Patrick would never say anything or be disloyal, I wanted to rescue him from the treacherous attention.

On the flight I'm imagining everything Paris has to offer and how I'll romance my lady. When Patrick and I arrive at the hotel, I'm surprised by Farrah's appearance. She looks haggard, and making matters worse, our son is cranky. So much for the return of the conquering hero. Tensions soon mount and will come to a head over a piece of chewing gum. Farrah is in the bathroom taking a shower. I'm groggy from jet lag, sitting on the bed with Patrick watching the World Cup on TV to relax. Patrick is chewing gum. Redmond, who was a toddler in 1986, wants some too, and like a fool I give him a piece. When Farrah comes out of the bathroom, she's incensed. It was beyond irresponsible of me. I obviously wasn't thinking. She rightfully becomes apoplectic. "He could have choked," she shouts. Patrick and I decide to give Farrah some space, so we go for a walk, hoping she'll have calmed down by the time we return. Though we manage to get through the last couple weeks on location without further incident, this event colors the rest of the trip for all of us.

All we can think about when *Nazi Hunter* wraps is returning to the familiar comforts of home. Our plans are deterred at the last minute. Tatum and John insist that on the way back to California, we stop over in New York for a visit at his parents' Long Island estate. I'd met his mother only briefly, at the hospital when Tatum was in labor, and I'd never met his father. But I don't want to hurt Tatum's feelings by declining and Farrah hasn't seen the baby yet, so with Patrick and little Redmond in tow, the four of us take a car from JFK to Oyster Bay. When we arrive, Tatum and John aren't there and his parents greet us with perplexed expressions. Soon I'm waiting for Alan Funt to pop out from a bush and say, "Surprise! You're on *Candid Camera*!" To this day, I remain convinced that John's parents were not expecting guests that afternoon.

Despite the awkward start, thanks to Farrah's unerring social grace, we spend a pleasant few days there, and then politely make our exit. And it's not only desperately missing home that's got me eager to leave. Several witnesses have come forward putting Griffin behind the wheel at the time of the accident, and my son needs his father. Two decades later, in her first book, Tatum will accuse Farrah and me of deliberately insulting John and his family with our abrupt departure. But that afternoon, as we're exchanging good-byes with the McEnroes, we think everything is hunky-dory.

Three months later an old boxing friend of mine calls and asks if Farrah and I would like to ride with them to the wedding. "What wedding?" I ask. "Tatum's," he replies. Now I know how John's parents must have felt when they saw us standing on their doorstep. Tatum had mentioned the possibility of marrying John. She and Farrah had even discussed wedding dresses. Sometimes they would sit on the stairs that led to the beach and talk and laugh. I could hear the conversations from my bedroom. Tatum would range between the girl asking advice from her big sister to a peer discussing men, marriage, and babies.

"John's parents want a big church wedding, but I'd rather do it on a surfboard on the beach," Tatum says.

"It's usually the other way around; it's the girl who wants the traditional celebration and the guy who wants to get it over with as fast as possible," Farrah replies.

"Maybe that's because he's a New Yorker and I'm a California beach girl," she answers.

"I've only known you a few years, but you've always been your own person, sometimes for better, sometimes for worse."

"It's been hard for me, Farrah."

"I know, Tatum, I know."

Over the past year, Farrah and Tatum have had talks like these, and never once did my daughter say anything about an actual wedding date. I tell myself it isn't true, that there has to be some mistake, that my daughter would never get married without her dad walking her down the aisle, without her grandparents sitting in the front row, proud of their only granddaughter and unable to imagine a more beautiful bride. I tell myself that, yes, Tatum and I have had our struggles, but she'd never be that callous, she'd never hurt her family that way. And I can think of nothing to precipitate such hateful behavior. There haven't been any blowups, no huge arguments, unless there was something smoldering beneath the surface, festering in that willful head of hers. I try to think of something I might have said or done, berating myself, then alternating to denial, convinced this is not so. I call my daughter and the machine picks up. I leave several messages. No response.

And then, The Telegram. It's dated August 1, 1986, 9:30 a.m. Pacific Daylight Time. And it reads:

I hold the yellow slip of paper in my hand, and the images begin flooding my memory: tossing a fifteen-month-old butterball into the air and catching her, delighting in her giggles; a ten-year-old Tatum meeting Sir John Gielgud in London, and curtsying when I whisper in her ear that he's a knight; that same girl watching me chat with Marlene Dietrich on an airplane and asking, "Daddy, who's that old lady?" I can hear Tatum and me rehearsing for *Paper Moon,* and her asking me to stop because she didn't want to get stale. She was nine years old. I see the two of us perched together on that yellow cardboard cutout of a half-moon, posing for the photograph that would illustrate the movie poster. Everyone assumes the photographer instructed her to pout for the photo. He didn't. She couldn't stand that itchy red taffeta dress Peter Bogdanovich, the director, made her wear that day. She was a precocious child. Hours on the set, takes and retakes, she rarely complained. I can still see little Addie Pray standing on that dusty country road, watching Mose drive away, and as the camera pulls back, she becomes smaller and smaller. In *Paper Moon* he comes back for Addie. Did I abandon the real girl on that dirt road? Or has she abandoned me?

When I found the telegram as I was reading some old papers refreshing my memory for this book, it made me relive the depths of disappointment all over again. A door inside me locked the morning that telegram came, and I am still blindly searching for the key to open it. I never knew which Tatum I was going to encounter, the warm, affectionate girl or the chilly worrisome young woman. Looking back now, Tatum and John also hurt themselves. The focus of the press coverage wasn't how beautiful the ceremony was or how glamorous the couple, but where were Ryan and Farrah? It shifted the conversation to family scandal, which was a shame. What still bothers me most was Tatum not inviting her grandparents. It's one thing for my daughter to want to punish Farrah and me, but it's another to do that to her grandparents. My mom and dad adored Tatum, were a loving, supportive presence in her life, and for them to be treated that way severed a bond between my daughter and me that has never been repaired.

Over the years, I often expressed my anger and frustration with Tatum to Farrah. She was never cold or unsympathetic. Early on she would listen to my woes about my children and offer reassurance, but eventually she would grow aloof. She had to in the interest of her own survival as well as our relationship. One day she sat me down and said, "Ryan, I can't be your whole world. It's not healthy. It's also not possible. We're both too dependent on each other, but I have a few close friends I can confide in. We shop, we gossip, we do lunch. You don't have anyone like that. The only grown-up men in your life are Freddie Fields and your father, and you can go to them for practical advice and they're helpful, but you don't talk to them about feelings, hopes, dreams. I love it that you trust me enough to tell me everything, but

I'm not a sage and at times I feel overwhelmed, inadequate, and I resent the fact that you ask too much and I'm only able to give too little." She was right and just as I didn't know what to say to Freddie or my dad when I was hurting, I didn't know what to say to Farrah then. I didn't want it to be different. I didn't want to need anyone but her. The two ends of our rainbow were no longer secured.

Before we're able to process the difficult events of the summer, autumn is upon us and duty calls. I've been cast in the Norman Mailer film *Tough Guys Don't Dance*, and I'll be on location in New England for a couple of months, after which I'll go to Maryland for Griffin's trial. Farrah will visit me briefly on set but she's busy preparing for *Poor Little Rich Girl*, the made-for-TV bio about Woolworth heiress Barbara Hutton, who had vast wealth and seven husbands but never found love. It's an elaborate production. They're shooting in London, Morocco, Los Angeles, and finishing in New York.

One of the luxuries of having a toddler is that you're able to travel as a family without having to worry about your child missing school. As soon as the holidays are over, Farrah, Redmond, and I, and Red's nanny, are on our way to London, ready for our next adventure. Before we even get out of the country, there's a Dickensian twist to our departure. We're in the air. We've just left Los Angeles International Airport. Suddenly, I feel the plane turning around. The pilot gets on the intercom and announces that we're rerouting the flight back to the airport for an emergency landing. There's an audible gasp in the cabin. Farrah's got Redmond in her lap. She tightens her grip on him. She is a soldier and a mother. While she may be terrified inside, nothing shows. Redmond picks up on her calmness and doesn't fuss. I reach over to check her seatbelt, and then give my own a good, strong tug. Farrah tightens her grip on Redmond. The woman sitting next to us pulls out a rosary, starts to pray. Some passengers are crying. Redmond's unaffected. He seems to think this is a fun new game. The pilot's voice booms over the intercom again. "Folks, we'll be using the emergency exit system today. Leave your carry-ons on board, and the flight attendants will direct you to the evacuation slides."

By now people are on the edge of hysteria. The plane makes its final descent and the wheels screech to a halt. The flight attendants pull open the emergency hatches, inflate the slides, and begin hustling everyone to the exit doors. I ease myself onto the slide, tuck Redmond firmly between my legs, and Farrah sits behind me, her arms and legs wrapped around me, and together our little family descends to the tarmac. "Again, again!" shouts Redmond. He thinks we're in Disneyland. We've been instructed to run as fast as we can to the ditch at the end of the runway. I hoist Redmond onto my shoulders, and the three of us scurry. We'll read about the reason for the emergency in the newspaper. Apparently the IRA notified police there was a bomb on board. This was during the Troubles in Belfast. A terrible business, but at least the Irish occasionally warn you first.

The next day we're back on board and up we go again. The bomb threat has upset Farrah. It's the first time I've seen her concerned about flying. So I take out the travel-size chess set that I'd brought along and teach her how to play, hoping it will keep her mind occupied. Not only does it distract her, but by the time we're making our approach into London's Heathrow Airport, she's checkmated me. I try to be a good loser. She loved that. Farrah was cunning, but when you're that pretty, people rarely give you any credit for your intelligence. Farrah had a keen mind. When she'd be handed a contract to sign, she'd review every line, and her questions would impress some of the best attorneys in the entertainment business. There was so much more to her than gleaming teeth and a bountiful head of hair. Farrah Fawcett wasn't beauty with brains, she was brains with beauty.

In London we're staying at Claridge's, a classy hotel near Hyde Park. The first night we're running through the TV channels when, to our surprise, we come across *Love Story*. With Redmond asleep beside us, Farrah and I watch it together for the first time, neither of us knowing how surely it predicts our future. Then again, the evening started out prophetically. A few hours earlier we'd called for room service and when our order arrived, as I was looking for my wallet, the guy dressed as a waiter suddenly has a camera aimed at us. He wouldn't stop. So I wrestled him out of our room. The incident was unsettling because someone must have helped this guy from the inside. I alerted the hotel manager, who was mortified and assured me that nothing like this would happen again. Wishful thinking. The next time we're so nakedly invaded will be twenty years later under horrific circumstances, when everything else Farrah and I will have endured will bear no comparison.

It doesn't take long for our family to return to our routine on location, though we do have an unexpected challenge the first few weeks. The nanny, a wonderful woman whom Redmond adores, injured her leg during our terrorism scare, and has to be excused for a while. So while Farrah's filming, I watch Redmond and bring him with me to the set as often as possible. Farrah owns her craft now, and I'm moved by that newly confident girl who still wants my judgment and opinion.

This production will prove even more physically taxing than the one in Paris. Farrah is portraying Barbara Hutton from youth through old age, and must endure long hours in the makeup chair each morning as a team of artists transforms her into a believable illusion of a woman at different stages of her life. Layers of latex, glue, and heavy pancake makeup are applied and reapplied until they achieve the desired effect. They must create molds of her head and face, which makes her look mummified. It makes me feel claustrophobic to watch. And then, after all that, her day starts, and she's got to act for eight to ten hours.

The public has romantic notions about being an actor, that we're constantly pampered and served. If you traveled with Farrah and me on location, you would see the truth of this life, and like us, I'm betting you, too, would have moments when you'd catch yourself looking for the nearest exit. I'm not saying there aren't some delicious perks. The best hotels, a car and a driver always at the ready, invitations to exclusive dinner parties, most of which we didn't attend because Farrah's schedule was so brutal, except of course in London, when we're asked to dine at the American ambassador's residence. But when you're away from home, simple acts such as driving yourself to work and buying your own groceries become the soothing routine that you desperately miss. And sometimes the longing for home can be overwhelming. When Redmond, who's teething, has kept us awake until the wee hours, I know as I watch Farrah leave our room in the morning that it's going to take everything she's got to hit her marks that day.

But now Farrah is the consummate pro. No matter how hard she's struggling, she shows up prepared and ready to work. Then she sheds the persona of Farrah Fawcett with all its burdensome complications, and slips into character, allowing the person she's portraying to enfold her, become her. It's one of the reasons she's so good in this part, and will be nominated for another Golden Globe. It makes me feel envious at times, but I'm glad that one of us can enjoy a respite from the train wreck I've made of my life. We both entered this relationship with baggage, but she brought a carry-on, and I came with a trunk.

To offset some of the stress, Farrah and I make the most of our time together on her days off: splashing with Redmond in the pool in Morocco; giving him his first swimming lesson; shopping at the casbah in Tangiers, Farrah relishing the market's exotic offerings, and me seeing her light up like a teenager when she successfully bargains a reasonable price for an intricate handwoven rug. I also take pleasure in doing little things for her. An inevitable reality of living in hotels is the exorbitant price of laundry. In some of these places, having underwear washed is more expensive than room service champagne. Neither Farrah nor I are cheap, but that feisty Texas girl in her doesn't like being taken advantage of. It's another of her qualities that I respect. I remember once she told me she got into a taxi in New York, and the cabbie tried to take the long way around to her destination. She demanded he stop the car and when he refused, she threatened him with her stiletto heel. So one day, while Farrah is on set, I gather all her delicates and wash them by hand as a surprise. When she gets back to the room and sees her bras and undies hanging neatly across the shower rod drying, she gives me an Eskimo kiss, then whispers in my ear why she loves me. It's one of the sweetest moments of the trip. Afterward, I would always pack a bottle of Woolite whenever we traveled.

In the years to come, I'll learn to string together those

moments like a strand of pearls that I can remove from the box and admire when I need to remind myself why this love is worth fighting for. I have to open that box some days more than others. After we return to London from North Africa, Farrah and I attend a fashion show, and the following morning, as I'm reading the paper over coffee, I come across an article that stops me cold. Here's an excerpt: "The 39-year-old former Charlie's Angel hopes the £10 million mini-series *Poor Little Rich Girl* will make her a TV star again. Ryan, whose career is in the doldrums and who looks after their two-year-old son Redmond while Farrah is filming, earned his keep this trip." Farrah is unfazed by the article and unsympathetic to my distress. Mean-spirited press doesn't affect her the way it does me. Not yet.

The article sets me off. It magnifies something I'm already dealing with privately: feeling emasculated. That night I'm supposed to join Farrah and some friends for dinner, but all I can think about is getting the hell out of London. So I do what any red-blooded male would in the same situation. I pick a fight with my woman, hoping I can piss her off just enough that she'll insist I leave. Instead I find this on the dresser:

DARLING RYAN,

I am terribly sorry that you're depressed but I feel
you are reacting to many things and the article just
compounds them. We are so strong together, things like

*this shouldn't touch us at this point in our love affair.
Your not wanting to come tonight has greatly affected
me. You are the life of any party and most certainly
always of mine. Tony's dinner at Tramp's is at 10:00,
and the theater isn't over until 10:30, so why don't you
go ahead and enjoy yourself without me until I arrive.
I seem to be the one depressing you and you'll have
more fun and I'm sure be greatly appreciated. Just be
happy and know that I love you more than ever, so
does Redmond. I thought we were the happiest family
ever. Am I wrong? Please don't leave me.*

FOREVER,

FARRAH

After reading the note, I stay. Wouldn't you?

By midsummer we're back in LA. Griffin is in trouble
again, this time for leading cops on a sixty-five-mile-
per-hour car chase through Beverly Hills. He's also remanded to jail for violating the terms of his probation on the
Gian-Carlo Coppola case, not having completed the court-
mandated community service hours. And my daughter in-
forms me via post that she isn't ready to see or talk to me
yet (I wasn't aware that we weren't speaking; this was news
to me) but will continue to send photos of my grandchild.
Two months later, on September 23, 1987, she gives birth to
another son, Sean McEnroe. I never knew she was pregnant.

The presence of her absence haunts me. With material like this, perhaps instead of being an actor, I should have become a playwright. Eugene O'Neill, stand clear.

Thank God I finally get a job to distract me from this long day's journey into despair. In *Chances Are,* a quirky romantic comedy about past lives, I play the new husband of Cybill Shepherd, whose dead husband, reincarnated by Robert Downey, Jr., falls in love with his own daughter, or something like that. Geez, I can't get away from this stuff. Anyhow, it's a cute movie. Robert is a warm and engaging fellow and I take an immediate liking to him. I witness his affinity for partying during production, and today I have reams of respect for him for having been able to turn his life around. If only my son Griffin could have done the same.

Looking back, I think it was during the filming of that picture that I began to recognize how much Farrah had changed me. We were staying on Antelo Road, and we were disagreeing about something, I don't remember what. I re-treated to the beach house in a huff. That evening I went out with Robert and his friends. Drugs and girls were ev-erywhere. It was anything goes. I couldn't wait to get back to Farrah. I didn't want that life. I didn't want to be free. I didn't want to chase women anymore. They were too easy to catch. So I called her and said, "May I come back?" And she said, "Of course." And when I pulled into the driveway, she was standing outside waiting for me. The old Ryan O'Neal would have dallied with every skirt in the place. Farrah was bringing out the better person in me, the man I wanted to become. Years later, I'd watch Robert being interviewed on ABC, confessing that his wife, Susan, had saved his life. I knew exactly what he meant.

Farrah and I also had a lot in common. For one thing, we were both athletic. Farrah's body-sculpting method was calisthenics. That woman could do one hundred deep side bends, push-ups, sit-ups, all the exercises that might be considered old-fashioned today. The results sure didn't look old-fashioned. I'd always been an active guy too, even owned a gym in Brentwood where bold-faced names worked out—Ali MacGraw, Jane Fonda, Mariel Hemingway, U2's Bono—a place where I enjoyed spending time and still do. We were also avid racquetball enthusiasts. Farrah's house on Antelo had a court. We'd spend hours playing racquetball or squash

Farrah and I battling it out on the racquetball court.

together. Farrah was a fierce competitor, graceful and power-ful. Some of my most vivid memories are of Farrah and me playing doubles. I often believed the teamwork we shared on the racquetball court would translate well on camera. That's why I accepted a surprise offer.

Farrah is on location in Canada with Redmond. She's in production for *Small Sacrifices,* a television miniseries based on the book by Anne Rule about a mother who tries to mur-der her children in a twisted attempt to win back her lover. I've just flown in from Vegas, where Griffin, surrounded by two or three dozen of his closest friends and former cell mates, got hitched, all expenses paid by yours truly. You may be wondering how Griffin could go from jail to mar-riage in a few short pages. If you're bewildered, try to imag-ine how it was for me.

Farrah and I have rented a sprawling ranch outside Ed-monton, Canada, with rolling hills and rural views. There are several horses being boarded on the property. Farrah thrives in this environment, and Redmond has his first horseback ride. One evening after work we're playing Ping-Pong (I put up a table and she's beating me every game), and she tells me, in between serves, that the producers still haven't cast the role of the lover, and would I be interested in playing him. Next, she places her paddle on the table, walks over to her purse, pulls out the script and hands it to me, and then leads me to the bedroom. Come morning, I'm learning my lines.

I was right about our on-camera chemistry. Farrah is as playful as she is erotic. There's this intimate scene where we're supposed to be engulfed in uncontrollable passion, so Farrah yanks off my belt and starts pulling my pants down. I blush and fumble my lines. The crew can't contain their laughter. She laughs, she flashes that heavenly smile, cocks her head, and says knowingly, "Too Texas for y'all?"

About a month later we're up at the house on Antelo, and Farrah is teaching me how to make chili. She's written out a list of ingredients without proportions. I'm standing there with an open can of chili powder in one hand, a quartet of measuring spoons in the other, and asking her how much to put in, and she says, "All great cooks improvise; they make the recipe their own. You're going to have to learn to trust your taste buds; it's a little bit like acting."

"Well, I don't like improvising," I say. "It's why I never took an acting class and why I always preferred to hang out with Bill Holden rather than James Dean." Farrah rolls her eyes. "I've been thinking about taking classes," she admits.

"I'm insulted. Why would you need classes when you have me as your coach," I say, only half in jest. She laughs. "Because almost everybody else we know, especially the ones from New York, take classes. They all feel it deepens their craft. It's the same way I feel about my art."

Farrah was an art major at the University of Texas and that's how she thought of herself, as a sculptor and a painter.

"I stumbled into acting because a publicist saw a photo

of me when I was in college and thought I could make a living as a model," she continues. "I never wanted to be an actress, and now that I'm successful I just wonder how much better I'd be if I actually got some training."

"You're a natural like me," I tell her. "Classes would only ruin it." I don't know if I even believed that at the time, but I've always been a little superstitious, and she was on such a roll that I honestly didn't think she needed anybody but me to help her refine her technique. And neither one of us had been conventionally ambitious. We cared without being driven. We took advantage of the opportunities that came along but rarely sought them. Mostly we just winged it. It almost always worked for us until it didn't.

When production wraps on *Small Sacrifices*, both Farrah and I are eager to work together again. So when *Saturday Night Live* alum Alan Zweibel and producer Bernie Brillstein approach me about starring in a new CBS sitcom parodying sports chat shows to begin production the following year, in 1990, I suggest Farrah for the female lead. I negotiate a good deal. In addition to getting paid seventy-five thousand dollars per episode, Farrah will also own a third of the show, which gives her a large participation in syndication revenue. In the sitcom business, that can mean serious money. Shows like *Seinfeld* and *Everybody Loves Raymond* generate more profit in reruns than they did with new seasons. Using Farrah benefits everyone. She gives the show what the industry calls marquee status, meaning star

appeal. The name of the show, with its dual meaning, is
Good Sports. Farrah portrays Gail Roberts, a former super-
model turned sports journalist. I play Bobby Tannen, a woe-
begone gridiron hero who couldn't resist the temptation of
women and booze. The premise is simple: we're cohosts of
a popular talk show on a network similar to ESPN. Apparently, we once had a fling. She remembers. I don't. Our
characters interview famous athletes who play themselves in
scenes that reveal hidden aspects of their actual lives. For
example, there's an episode with football Hall of Famer Jim
Brown in which he recounts his childhood ambition to become a harpist. And there's another with the owner of the
New York Yankees, George Steinbrenner, about his chicken
farm in Florida. Farrah plays the bright one. I play the dim
one. What could go wrong?

CHAPTER FIVE

BAD SPORTS

Writing a book is an emotional odyssey, sometimes exhilarating, other times deflating. Today I'm trapped in the latter, having to confront certain truths about Farrah. Writing about *Good Sports* in the previous chapter brought it back to me, this conversation Farrah and I had.

It was right after we had taped our last show. Farrah and I were vacationing in the Bahamas. We were having dinner at a highly recommended little restaurant on the water. A handsome couple was sitting across from us. And Farrah says to me, "I've been watching those people since we sat down. They don't even look at each other. Who has dinner and doesn't speak?" I said, "Married people." I got that line from somewhere, and though I didn't remember then, I do now. The dialogue was from the 1967 movie *Two for the Road* with Audrey Hepburn and Albert Finney. It's the story of a married couple told through a series of flashbacks that recaptures the trips that punctuate their life together. These scenes take the audience through the universal stages of every long-term relationship: love in the beginning, at its most idyllic; the baby years when responsibility eclipses romance; the inevitable disillusionment of familiarity; and then, the ennui that either swallows you or that you both choke back and conquer. I'm making this superb movie sound more cynical than it is. Probably just my state of mind, thinking about all this and not having another chance, like Hepburn and Finney, to make it right.

Anyhow, in *Two for the Road* there's this clever motif the screenwriter uses as a commentary on what happens when two people are together for a long time. It's up to the audience to determine whether the message is optimistic or cautionary. At various intervals on the road, Hepburn and Finney will encounter a couple dining together in silence, and when Hepburn asks what sort of people sit together and don't talk to each other, Finney says, "Married people." Was it the silence of two people so comfortable with each other that they don't feel the need to say anything; or was it a stony silence, born of frustration or, worse, indifference?

I rented the movie today and I've been sitting here watching it. The last time I saw *Two for the Road* was with Farrah. We laughed at all the witty parts. I'm not laughing now.

Just like those couples in the movie, at some point the conversation between Farrah and me stopped. It's as if our love was put on mute. We could see and touch each other, read each other's moods like fingers tracing across braille, but our mechanism for reconciling, for flushing the toxins out of the relationship, had atrophied. I never realized it until I began this book and started viewing my memories with a new lens, not an easy thing to do when those memories are all you have left. What I'm about to tell you I've never admitted to anyone, not even to myself. The truth is I believe the conversation Farrah and I began that first long-ago weekend in Big Sur, where we talked for days about everything important, luxuriating in the joy of getting to know each other, stopped that autumn of 1990 when *Good Sports* started taping its first and only season.

I can see it as if I were watching a movie trailer. Pushing Farrah beyond comfort; convincing myself it's for her own good, like a personal trainer so focused on results that he doesn't realize he's put too much strain on his charge's joints; an insecure Farrah, whose hands are sweating and whose throat becomes tight trying to be funny on cue; the endless production meetings; the rigid rehearsal schedules and strained performances; the live studio audiences; the conflicts with producers; the constant scrutiny of the press; the flat scripts; the nagging questions: Will we be picked up for another season? Will the network give us a better time slot? Flashback to a younger Ryan and Farrah in Big Sur as they slip into the Jacuzzi and kiss; close-up of that same couple a decade later, returning home in LA after fourteen hours on the set of *Good Sports,* climbing into opposite ends of the Jacuzzi and reviewing next week's script in silence, then retiring to separate bedrooms, where one will escape into sleep, and the other will write in his journal all the things he should be telling her but doesn't.

JOURNAL ENTRY, NOVEMBER 7, 1990

There is this thin, impenetrable veil between us.
We're professional and considerate to each other on
the set; cool, almost aloof at home. Farrah told me
today that we remind her of Jack and Anjelica. They
loved each other but it wasn't enough for Nicholson.
She accuses me of being bored and angry. Maybe
she's right. Sometimes our love just doesn't make up
the differences. I constantly hesitate. I feel like the
guy who wants to prove he can go over Niagara Falls
but is afraid to get in the barrel.

Yes, we were sleeping in separate bedrooms by then, but not for the reasons you're thinking. When Redmond was a toddler he'd come into our bedroom at night wanting to sleep between us. Redmond has strong legs like his mother, and he would burrow into the bed, decide he didn't have enough room, and then start pushing with all his might, until I had no other choice but to sleep on the floor or in the other room. Eventually he outgrew this, but by then, Farrah and I had grown used to our privacy and it stuck, and even when we traveled after that, we'd often get adjoining rooms. I always thought of our arrangement as terribly mature of us. Now I wish I could have back every one of those nights we slept in separate beds.

Today at the beginning of the second decade of the new

century, I feel like an archaeologist sifting through the artifacts of his own life, trying to decipher answers to questions that keep changing with every new discovery. I recently stumbled across an original transcript of a magazine interview that Farrah and I must have done together in late 1990 when *Good Sports* was in production. I'd never seen it before. It's missing the title page and I found it stuffed in the back of a box full of old financial statements. I started reading. "My parents were upset when I moved in with Lee," Farrah is quoted. "They made me feel so bad about myself. They forced me into that marriage." And Lee would encourage her subservience in their relationship. Now Farrah must have felt she was losing control all over again, little by little, bit by bit. *Good Sports* was only part of it.

Farrah saw herself at everyone's mercy: me; the network; audiences; our family; my children; her own body, which was beginning to rebel with recurring maladies: headaches, sinus infections, strep throat. And then menopause. It was nature unleashed, and Farrah was headed toward the eye of that storm. Of course neither one of us understood it at the time. You'd think we would have been aware of the change in temperature between us, but we'd always been and remained a passionate, volatile couple. Even when we weren't speaking to each other, the sex was tender and satisfying, perhaps because we never used it as a weapon, never punished one another by withholding affection. We were as much alive when we fought as we were when we made love.

We assumed it was our nature, that fluctuations in the atmosphere had become a normal part of who we were together. Besides, who pays attention to storms that hit fast and then dissipate? It's the ones the meteorologists warn you about, the ones with first names that you prepare for. Farrah and I had been a couple for more than ten years at this time. We'd weathered Hurricane Tatum, Griffin the tornado, my career drought, and the vicious journalistic hail the size of golf balls that dented both our egos. The question I ask myself now is at what point should a couple say to themselves: the way in which we survive these assaults isn't healthy.

Sifting through all of this memorabilia, I've found trunks of letters between Farrah and me, some are written on napkins, others across the pages of day-old newspapers. Anything we could find to write on, we'd jot these notes to each other. Some of them are loving little mementos, where I'm letting Farrah know that I've gone to the gym and that I already miss her.

Others are notes from Farrah to me or to Redmond, reminding me to pick up the dry cleaning, or him to be sure to finish his spelling homework.

Then there are the letters hastily scribbled in the wake of an argument, as well as the apologies, some of which I couldn't bear to finish in one sitting. I had to read them in stages, lest regret consume the strength I need to continue with this book. To quote the great Irish playwright Samuel Beckett, "I can't go on I'll go on."

11 AM

P. RYAN O'NEAL

Dear one —
I've discussed with ZiZA
the parking, The Gates, The Garage
etc. I'm off to see the wizard about
your cleaning + my Gym, Davey Dog's
bones and then I'll pick up your
beautiful son Redmond. I hope that
Life is beautiful for you Tetey and if
you need me for anything just give me
a call.
       forever PRO

My full name is Patrick Ryan O'Neal. PRO are my initials
and that's how I sign every casual letter and note.

Redmond,
You MUST bring
home your words
and handwriting.
home!
Please remember.

I Love you with
all my heart. ♡
You need to do
your Phonics this
morning — And your
#3 in the gold book →

Just read it
over and we'll
memorize it
tomorrow.

Be good and Kind,
and concentrate
in class.

Kisses,

& You are the
best !!!

Mommie.

Sitting here is making me realize that it wasn't just Farrah edging toward losing control, though she was the one bearing the brunt; we were both untethered. We navigated our way past the turmoil through notes, letters, racquetball, sex, and I had my journal. All those devices are perfectly fine to enrich communication, but none of them are substitutes for an open conversation. Farrah and I became so acclimated to an elaborate system of evasion that it made us believe everything was okay. I don't think either one of us was consciously aware that we were floating free, but Farrah's moods made it apparent she knew that somewhere inside her she was shrinking.

During production on *Good Sports*, Farrah was more

amorous and adventuresome than ever. I had forgotten about that until I saw a reference to it in one of my journals, and it gave me pause.

JOURNAL ENTRY, FEBRUARY 21, 1991

I'm waiting for my poster girl. My most perfect lover. She is so willing to experiment lately. I have to reach back for retired fantasies.

I suspect she became more sexual because that was the one area where she had complete confidence. I'm not sure I'd agree that we didn't communicate at all. We did, but it was like playing connect the dots with a pencil whose tip kept breaking.

I also overstepped my role as her mentor, and what started out as a mutually rewarding exchange evolved into something harmful. One morning I'm making my way downstairs from my bedroom and I hear Farrah on the phone in the living room. I stop and listen. I'm not sure whom she's talking with, but it's got to be a friend or a confidante. "He's giving me too many instructions. It's too much. He even tells me when to blink my eyes. I know he wants to help, but I can't handle two directors at once. I'm afraid to say anything because it's so important to him." I retreat to my bedroom unnoticed.

In my defense, I had only Farrah's best interests at

heart. What Ryan "Henry Higgins" O'Neal lost sight of was that it was one thing to encourage Farrah to take on challenges she was excited to try and another to push her into a situation that made her desperately insecure. *Good Sports* must have made her feel like a spectator in her own life. No wonder she rebelled.

So where were we? Oh yes, the end of 1990. The Christmas holidays give us a much-needed break from the show. We're able to shed the skins of Gail Roberts and Bobby Tannen and just be Farrah and Ryan. There's a misconception about celebrities and holidays: that we are guaranteed a sprinkling of yuletide fairy dust that civilians aren't. I assure you that holidays, at least for us, could be as messy and wonderful, frustrating and joyous, unpredictable and mundane as they are for everyone else. Our Christmas and New Year's consisted of family rituals we'd developed over years of putting up Christmas trees, sneaking peeks inside the tiny doors on Advent calendars with our son, and hiding presents in closets. Farrah's mom and dad spent many Christmases with us after Redmond was born and that year was no exception. They provided a dose of normal in a household desperately in need of it. I'd come home from the gym and find Farrah's dad, Jimbo, sitting on the couch with his grandson in his lap, reading him *The Night Before Christmas*; or Farrah helping Redmond hang the Christmas stockings over the fireplace; or her mom, Pauline, who seemed to mellow at Christmastime, taking a roast out of the oven while Farrah set the table. I didn't just commit these images to memory, I absorbed them, knowing they were moments I'd one day need to revisit.

Friday night, January 11, 1991, 10 p.m., *Good Sports* premieres. The critics are dissecting our "surprising lack of on-air chemistry." Worse, the ratings are dismal. Doesn't anyone remember that *Small Sacrifices* was nominated for an Emmy and a Golden Globe? But that's how this industry works. You're only as good as your last success, and as far as the reviewers and the network are concerned, that miniseries is ancient history. The public is fickle too. Consider Charlie Sheen. One day he's the sitcom leader in television land who becomes a hero across America; the next day he's a nut making a spectacle of himself spewing nonsense on prime time who can't give away tickets to his Torpedo of malarkey tour. Six months later everyone loves him again after a brilliantly self-deprecating interview on Jay Leno. Good for you, Charlie!

While Farrah and I are still trying to catch our breath from the disappointing premiere, we're hit with another setback. This time, it's not Tatum; it's her husband, John. The producers of *Good Sports* thought I could persuade McEnroe to appear in an episode. They'd already roughed out a script that they asked me to give to him. I believed it would be good for John's career, but even more important, I thought it was a wonderful opportunity for my son-in-law and me to mend fences that had been in a state of disrepair since that weekend five years earlier at his parents' house. Though Farrah and I did see John and Tatum on occasion, it was always awkward, and by the middle of an evening everyone would be making excuses about why it was time to go (sadly I rarely saw my grandchildren and I wouldn't really start to know them until years later when Tatum and I began our reality show). I was hopeful that if John did an episode of *Good Sports*, it might quell the dissonance. No such luck. I never even hear back from him, not a word. I call, I leave messages. I send Patrick, who's staying in New York, to hand deliver the script. To this day, John has yet to acknowledge the offer. On a personal level, it was hurtful. Professionally, it was humiliating.

One of the bright spots of the winter is our darling son's sixth birthday, on January 30, 1991. We give him a golden retriever puppy as his present. We name him Davey Dog. He becomes a member of the family. Davey lived a happy life with us until old age finally took him at fifteen. He was my friend and constant companion. I enjoyed bathing and brushing him and bringing him treats from the doggie health food store. I grew up with dogs. My parents had collies. To me, the love of a pet is an essential part of life; without it, something important is missing. I have Mozart now. He's a mixed breed. I adopted him from Best Friends Animal Sanctuary. He's all fuzz and personality. I think he may even have a future in television. He's appeared in several episodes of the reality show with Tatum and me and the camera seems to love him. Farrah was a dog lover too. When her beloved Afghan, Satchel, died, she called me from the vet's. She was sobbing. I said, "I'm on my way." She said, "No, we're coming home, wait for us." I said, "We?" She replied, "Satchel and me." The vet wanted to dispose of him, but Farrah wouldn't hear of it. Instead, she wrapped him in a blanket and brought him back to the house on Antelo, where we buried him together. Mariah Carey is living on that piece of property now. I wonder if I should warn her not to dig a garden in the northwest corner of the lot.

As the year progresses, there's a steady, subtle decline in Farrah's demeanor. She's moody and restless and her headaches have graduated to migraines. She's showing up late to the set and is easily distracted. I have the network discontinue the live audience, thinking it will make her less self-conscious about her comic timing. I'm searching, trying to figure out what's wrong. A cynical woman has replaced the cheerful, optimistic girl I fell in love with.

JOURNAL ENTRY, MARCH 4, 1991
FF isn't her best today. Another difficult period.
Bleeding. Hurting. Forgetting her lines. Although she
manages to look smashing through it all. I'm still
in love with Ms. Texas. Redmond is at the movies
with the babysitter and I'm waiting patiently for
his return. He now only wants to snuggle with me.

His mother said, "Life is shit." Maybe she just needs some room to breathe.

What she needed was for me to be patient with her, re-assure her that Redmond wasn't choosing me over her, that it was normal and healthy for a boy that age to want to spend more time with his dad. But I'm a man and don't think in those terms. I assumed she'd welcome the peace and quiet. I know she wasn't jealous. She must have felt spurned. I still remember the expression on her face when she'd come to collect Redmond, who was sleeping on my lap, for bed, and he'd plead to be left where he was. Most every night I'd have to carry him upstairs and tuck him in. I probably should have read the copy of *Men Are from Mars, Women Are from Venus* that Farrah gave me for my birthday. And both of us should have worked at achieving a balance in our parenting styles instead of bringing the same competition we enjoyed on the racquetball court into our raising of Redmond. It wasn't anything we did consciously, but Redmond sensed it. When I wrote the above journal entry, all I thought I knew was that Farrah was too strict with our son and that she needed to relax with him the same way she needed to loosen up at work. While I may have had a valid point, I'm realizing now that there was more to Farrah's concern about discipline than her conservative Catholic roots or all the parenting classes she took.

She was scared to death.

We'd have arguments about how to set boundaries for Redmond: bedtime; food; respecting adults; and most vital, why rules must be obeyed. I'd defend myself by saying that I'd raised three children, that I was the experienced parent, not her. And that's exactly what worried her. Griffin must have been a specter haunting her peace of mind, and if she was too tough on Redmond sometimes, if her voice did go shrill when she saw him doing something he shouldn't, it was because she wanted to protect her son from a fate like his brother's. The problem was that the stricter she was with Redmond, the less influence she had over him. A therapist could have figured this out, but Farrah and I never consulted one. My only experience with a counselor had been with Tatum when she was a teen. It was such a disaster that it soured me on the entire profession. And Farrah was a private person, reluctant to reveal herself to any stranger.

Our clashes over Redmond escalate and our fighting takes a revelatory turn. It's not so much that's it's getting more severe as it is stripping us psychologically naked, removing all pretense from our relationship. We're discovering that those same two people who once brought out the best in each other also have a frightening capacity for bringing out the worst. I remember one afternoon when we're in the car. I said something to set her off and she starts yelling at me, which I detest, so I simply ignore her. Next thing I know, her foot is in my face and she's pushing it into my cheek as I'm driving up Benedict Canyon, all because I wouldn't buckle under to her demands for disciplining our son. I was no Mahatma Gandhi either. Once, she locked herself in the bathroom and I punched my fist through the door. A piece of wood hit her in the face, cutting her above the eye. I broke a knuckle. So picture the two of us, she's bleeding and I've got an ice pack on my hand. We're both apologizing and trying not to cry. I should have recognized that none of this was normal, but after what I'd gone through with Joanna Moore, it seemed almost tame.

It was now fall, and we were swatting away disappointments like picnickers harassed by mosquitoes: Tatum gives birth to a daughter but says nothing; *Good Sports* gets canceled; Griffin is arrested again. And the elementary school we want for Redmond rejects our application. Aaron Spelling is on the board of trustees.

We start taking it out on each other.

And then the incident.

Farrah and I are in my room. We're quietly quarreling. It devolves into a shouting match. Suddenly our six-year-old son is standing in the doorway in his Winnie-the-Pooh pajamas, staring at us. He's holding a butcher knife. He must have climbed onto a chair and pulled the knife out of the rack on the kitchen counter. He points the tip of the blade at his chest. "I'm gonna stab myself if you don't stop it!"

That ended the argument.

For the next hour we sat with our little boy on either side of his bed, soothing him. We told happy funny stories and when he finally began to laugh, Farrah and I embraced, assuring him that we loved each other and he was safe.

We should have run to a family therapist's office the very next day.

Instead I'd run to Vancouver.

Neither Farrah nor I ever acknowledged that this behavior should not have been acceptable in our family. One of us should have been the grown-up. Instead, we were two single-minded people who gave in to our baser impulses, making excuses for each other when we felt forgiving, and baiting each other when we didn't. Our moral compass had become submerged in a sea of ego and confusion, and our sweet little boy would bear the brunt of the corrosion. He would become increasingly recalcitrant and distracted: he'd open a drawer and forget to close it; he'd lose everything, from his catcher's mitt to his favorite pen. At school he wouldn't make friends. Afternoons when I picked him up, I'd either find him sitting by himself or running aimlessly around the playground.

There's an old expression: "When you're young, the days fly and the years drag; when you're older, the days drag and the years fly." It's true of relationships too. And oh how the days dragged for both Farrah and me during this period! Vancouver becomes a welcome escape. It's now 1992. I'm on location shooting the made-for-TV movie *The Man Upstairs* with Katharine Hepburn. It's about the unlikely friendship that blossoms between a lonely, elderly woman and the escaped convict whom she discovers hiding in her attic. The script was developed for Katharine, and my old buddy Burt Reynolds is executive producing. Originally he was going to star in it too, but scheduling conflicts force him to assign the role to someone else, and I'm grateful

he chooses me. Working with Katharine Hepburn is akin to being knighted by the queen. On set, she has a benevolent regality that puts you at ease while making you want to stand up a little bit straighter. I'd heard a lot about Katharine Hepburn when I was growing up in Holly-

wood, but I'd never met her. I discover she's not the reclusive eccentric now depicted by the press. Though protective of her privacy, she's intelligent and witty, with an endearing practical side. Unlike some movie stars who fight the aging process one plastic surgeon at a time, Katharine Hepburn's beauty is preserved in the sanctuary of her dignity, untouched and untouchable.

Farrah and Redmond come for a few days. The recent

time apart proves a blessing as the tensions prior to my departure have quelled, and both Farrah and I strive to keep things polite and casual. For some women, diamonds are forever. For Farrah, it's Mexican food. I've made arrangements with the hotel chef to serve all her favorite south-of-the-border dishes. There's a buffet waiting in the room when she arrives. Redmond is delighted and Farrah is touched.

One of the highlights of their visit is Redmond's foray into the world of special effects. *The Man Upstairs* is a Christmas movie. If you rent it, pay attention to the scene in which Katharine and I walk outside when it's snowing. Notice how real it looks. Redmond was expertly tossing that fake snow down on us.

I also remember introducing Katharine to Farrah. It's like a meeting of the goddesses. Farrah is quiet and deferential. Though she'd been in the presence of other greats, Katharine Hepburn made you catch your breath. She invites Farrah and me to her house for tea. She sends her driver of forty years to fetch us. Her housekeeper, a lovely lady who looks to be further along in years than Katharine, greets us at the door. This is Katharine Hepburn's entourage, two sweet ancients whom she clearly cares about and who are devoted to her in turn. Katharine is a gracious host and an engaging conversationalist. In the car on the way back, Farrah puts her head on my shoulder and drifts off to sleep. I can feel the warmth of her breath on my neck, as I did on that long ago drive from Disney Ranch, and it makes me yearn to regain the ease of those early years together. Then I think of Katharine Hepburn and that moment when she stared into the distance and began talking to Farrah and me about Spencer Tracy, and those strong shoulders slumped ever so slightly. She still missed him, as I miss Farrah today. They never married either.

Years later, Farrah would tell me that after she saw my reverence for Katharine, she understood why I watched classic movies and had such respect not just for the actors in the studio system, but for the craft itself, the directors, and the cinematographers, and that she was proud to have the same profession as Miss Hepburn, as she insisted on addressing Katharine. It comforts me to know that Farrah never regretted becoming an actress, because there were periods in our life when I worried she wished she had never left Texas. By the time 1992 rolled to a close, I'd be worried again.

And it's Griffin who rings the bell for the next round. It's December and I've just arrived at the courthouse for his sentencing. I want to offer my moral support. Remember I told you he was arrested again? It was for firing shots at his ex-girlfriend's unoccupied car. Moral support? That's like putting spit on an amputation, but I had to keep trying with Griffin. I'm not sure whether it was love or guilt that compelled me to keep giving him another chance, but he was my son, and back then I could no more turn my back on him than my dad, Blackie, could have turned his on me. I won't always feel that way. If you're wondering what happened to the wife from the wedding I paid for in Vegas, they had a child, then a scandalous divorce. I find out that right before I arrive at the courthouse, my ex-wife Joanna, who had just been there to wish her son luck, rolled her car over four times on the freeway. While the judge was handing down Griffin's sentence, his mother was being cut out of the wreckage. She had two fingers severed and had to undergo emergency surgery. She was fortunate to be alive. But that woman had been cheating death since I'd known her. When we were first married, I came home one night to find her passed out in a bathtub with an open bottle of barbiturates and a tumbler of wine on the side of the tub. It took me more than an hour to wake her. Joanna was the worst decision I ever made, but I bear her no ill will. I was a kid when we got hitched and back then no one understood much about addiction. Her accident shakes me. It could just as easily have been Griffin. I remember thinking at the time that Tatum may have been a challenge, but thank God she wasn't throwing away her life like her mother and her brother were.

When I get home that night, I wear my anxiety like a vest, expecting Farrah to gently remove it and make me presentable again. But she's dealing with her own demons. Another headache, another spotty period, another dark mood. Everything annoys her. There's too much traffic on the PCH. The fog isn't burning off until noon. Anything I suggest to cheer her she rejects, convinced it will just make matters worse. I offer a sentimental journey to the Pierre Hotel in New York. I even book the same room we had in the early days when I was introducing Farrah to the city. It's where we became a couple and began to think of ourselves as a unit, inseparable, joined together not only as lovers but as partners. We'd made a pact. And we believed in it back then. The Pierre's neighborhood, Fifth Avenue at Sixty-first Street, the storied Plaza Hotel across the way, and the fountain where Scott and Zelda Fitzgerald once danced are still eternal New York. Maybe we can, as the jazzman once said, get our mojo back. Good memories remain, enough to soften the bad ones. Andy Warhol's gone six years now and Studio 54 was shuttered a couple of summers ago, but Central Park is just across the street and the stores on Madison Avenue begin a block east. We'll sneak back to the attic if it hasn't been converted to apartments. There may be a cherub left, one more for luck. She says the last thing she wants to do is get on an airplane. I go upstairs and reluctantly call our hotel in New York. I can hear the Pierre manager's disappointment. "I'm sorry too," I say. "More than you know." As the weeks turn to months, we struggle to find our footing. It's as if Farrah and I are entwined in a dance with no choreography.

I'm sitting here reading through my journal entries for 1993. Professionally, I don't see much. There's a singsong quality to these pages. I go to the gym; I coach Redmond's Little League team; he misses a pop-up; he catches a pop-up; he does his homework; he doesn't do his homework;

he mouths off; he's good as gold; Davey Dog needs biscuits; I pay my taxes; I lament my knees. Then . . . wait a minute, this can't be right.

JOURNAL ENTRY, MARCH 3, 1993
A sweetheart of a day except for poor FF and her weekly migraine.

When did she start getting migraines every week?

JOURNAL ENTRY, MARCH 30, 1993
Hard to get going this morning. Poor Farrah, who can hardly move from this terrible flu, just lies in her bed. I wish I could help her take it. This is the third time this month.

JOURNAL ENTRY, APRIL 19, 1993
Farrah's sick again. Her mom's here cooking dinner. I've been taking on more and more with Redmond. Farrah needs the break.

I don't remember Farrah's being so sick that we needed her mom to stay and help.

JOURNAL ENTRY, APRIL 27, 1993
When I came back from my run, Farrah was gone. I go to the gym as usual and pick up my son from

school. Then it's homework and play-offs. As
for his mom, she's sick again and already in bed.
I bathe him and help him brush his teeth, then
tuck him in.

I must have been in another world. It was right there
staring at me and I kept on going about my daily routines
as if everything was copacetic. Now it's coming back to me.
Pauline and Jimbo had come for the holidays, as they did
most years. But Farrah was poorly and so Pauline decided
to stay on and help out. And I remember now how much she
missed Jimbo. She never would have stayed that long unless
she was concerned for her daughter. But did I ever ask her
why she was worried about Farrah? Did I ask her whether
I should be just as worried? All those years I resented my
mother-in-law's intrusion in our lives when I should have
been working with her to help the girl we both loved so desperately. Pauline, if you can hear me, I'm sorry. I'm so, so
sorry.

And then the journal entries stop. Maybe the rest
of that year is somewhere here at the beach house and I
haven't found it yet. Or maybe things got so much worse
that I couldn't write about them anymore. I'm not sure. I remember that year in bits and pieces. Don't believe what the
New Age gurus tell you. Enlightenment doesn't stomp in; it
comes on tiptoes.

All I remember next is the earthquake . . .

CHAPTER SIX

FAULT LINES

The earthquake of 1994 that splintered West LA felt like the ground was speaking in tongues, telling all of us who lived and worked there that maybe the jig was up, that the greed and hubris, the atavistic culture—that wellspring for innumerable movies, television shows, mediocre books, and submediocre plays that had come to define much of Southern California in its glory years—were over. The earth roared and swallowed people's homes, their businesses, their golf courses, their closets full of shoes. It was as if God were telling us off. The quake struck LA at 4:30 a.m. on January 17. It may have been a natural disaster, but it would become a preternatural metaphor for what was happening to Farrah and me.

Seismic shifting.

Tremors beneath the surface.

A cracking foundation.

It's something out of a movie. I wake up to a bookcase crashing onto the bed. The third volume of the 1960 *Britannica* struck me square on the forehead. Redmond is in his room at the other end of the hall. Farrah's away at a New Age retreat. It's pitch-black. I hear a deep low rumbling and

the rattle of lamps and knickknacks shaking on the tabletops
and the thud of boxes tumbling off the shelves in Farrah's
massive walk-in closet. I grab the flashlight I keep in the bed
stand and make my way to Redmond. I'm stepping through
broken glass. There are pictures of Farrah strewn across the
floor. The frames have broken. I see Redmond standing in
the corner with his hand on his heart. "Burglar, burglar!" he
cries. He doesn't realize it's me. "No, Redmond, it's Dad."
I tell him there's been an earthquake. "Are there going to be
aftershaves?" he asks.

Together we gingerly make our way down the hall. The
house is collapsing around us. Paintings that hung on the
walls appear as if they're flinging themselves out of harm's
way, just as someone might jump out of a window in a burning building. Everything is moving. When we get to the living room, that's when we see it, the fissure that starts at the
front entryway and goes through the kitchen, out the back
door, through the alley, and into our neighbor's tennis court.
I point the flashlight down, and Redmond and I follow it like
the yellow brick road to hell. It's wide enough that you could
fall through the crack and when you look into it, there's no
bottom, no Emerald City. As I'm snapping Polaroids, an
aftershock hits that knocks Redmond and me off our feet.
We head for the car. Wilt Chamberlain lives next door and I
watch as the enormous leaded windows that frame the entire
front of his home explode onto his lawn. Then I see his large
silhouette pulling open the gates to his driveway because the

electricity is out. Everything's out. He slides into his car and revs the engine. He wants to flee. But there's a leaking gas line. He's about to drive over it. I frantically wave my hands, shouting that it's too dangerous. I tell him to turn off his engine, which he does, and Redmond and I push him safely to the other side of the street. He drives off without a word.

Redmond and I wait for the "aftershaves" to pass. (Don't worry, Davey Dog was safe and sound at the beach house with friends.) By daybreak, we're on the road to San Diego to pick up Farrah, who's been caught up in the spiritual growth movement, which in 1994 was rampaging. She's a seeker. She's bought into a lingo that preaches everyone has a destiny and a purpose and it's possible to find it. I'm skeptical.

Driving through the epicenter, the scene unfolding before us resembles some prehistoric apocalypse. When we arrive at Deepak Chopra's retreat where Farrah has spent the week, she can't understand why we've come. I try to tell her that the house on Antelo is destroyed, but she doesn't quite believe me. I show her the Polaroids. "It doesn't look that bad to me," she says. But when Redmond and I finish describing what we'd just witnessed, Farrah is convinced.

Farrah's beloved house on Antelo is red tagged, declared unlivable. The street had collapsed and the house had slipped off its moorings, half of it sliding to the hillside below. It will cost hundreds of thousands of dollars to set the wounded structure on new pilings and bring the building up to code. The insurance company officially cites the cause of destruction as a "prehistoric landslide," which somehow isn't covered under her policy. Farrah is devastated. That house on Antelo was more to Farrah than mere brick and mortar. It represented her survival of an unhappy marriage; her rebirth as an independent woman; her safe place; her proof that no man got the best of her—not Lee Majors, not me at my best or at my worst—proof that she was her own master. When the house crumbled, it was as if her independence, her strength and resolve, even her resiliency, crumbled with it. As neighbors combed through the wreckage of what were once their homes, Farrah was sifting through the wreckage inside her self, her spirit as severed as the pilings.

We decide to move into the smaller house next door, which we had bought several years earlier as a guesthouse, and which remarkably had withstood the earthquake. We lease a place in Coldwater Canyon while it's being remodeled. What neither of us realizes is that the fissure that split the Antelo house in two won't be the only structural crack we can't fix, that soon Farrah and I will find ourselves trying to rebuild a relationship across a widening chasm equally as deep. By the time spring arrives, Farrah and I are both teetering on the edge of falling in, but instead of reaching out hands to offer support, we're giving each other little shoves.

We disagree about when the plumber was supposed to arrive, who forgot to buy the kiwi, or who left the prescriptions at the pharmacy. She blames me when Redmond receives a D on a spelling quiz because it was my turn to help him study. I ask how it is possible she didn't remember to turn on the Jacuzzi. She yells at me for rushing her. I get sarcastic when she takes too long to get ready. On and on it goes, a dreadful call and response that transforms the innocuous into the inescapable.

There's a legend that famous couples never quarrel over such plebeian concerns as whose turn it is to fire the housekeeper. While it's true some celebrities can be self-indulgent, most of us lead lives that are more like yours than you think. And we're no more immune than you from getting stuck for hours waiting for the cable guy or confusing the day we're scheduled to take the dog to the vet. The public's misconceptions about celebrity have always amused me. I was at the market the other day (yes, I buy my own groceries) standing in line at the checkout counter, and I began thumbing through one of those personality magazines and came across an article titled "They're Just Like Us." It featured a photo of a disheveled Cameron Diaz gulping down a cup of coffee, and a sweaty Jennifer Aniston, damp hair pasted to her forehead, exiting the gym. I think they ran a shot of Farrah and me playing Frisbee several years back. So many of the people who read these rags fantasize about living the life of a star, never realizing that some celebrities wish they could change places with them. Farrah told me that she had dreams about what it would be like to lead a life without the frenzy of renown, to share a home with a stable husband and be a regular mom, active in the local community, a member of the PTA. "In my dreams there are all these white picket fences," she once said. "Sometimes they're chasing me down a suburban street and I'm frightened. Other times they surround me and I feel safe and secure. I'm waiting for somebody. I think it's you."

The yearning for normalcy usually parallels the trajectory of one's fame. For Farrah, I think it started in Paris on location for *Nazi Hunter,* and by the time we were living in Coldwater Canyon, I could sense that longing growing larger within her, making her want to escape from everything.

Speaking of wanting to escape, I just got home from New York, where Tatum and I did the publicity junket for our reality show. And I thought the LA earthquake was a disaster!

B ack to 1994. It's late spring. Farrah is in Vancouver filming *Man of the House* with Chevy Chase, a lighthearted Disney comedy about a boy who doesn't want a new stepfather in his territory. I've just landed a role in the movie *Faithful,* with Cher and Chazz Palminteri. Directed by my old chum Paul Mazursky, it's a black comedy about a wife who turns the tables on her husband who's hired a hit man to knock her off. I'm the husband. For some bewildering reason Paul Mazursky reminds me of Barbra Streisand, both interesting filmmakers. It helped that I had worked with Streisand before I did *Barry Lyndon* with Stanley Kubrick. They

had the same work ethic, perfectionists and as demanding on themselves as they were on the cast and crew.

Faithful is being filmed on location in New York and I decide to visit Farrah in Vancouver on my roundabout way to the East Coast. It will almost prove the unraveling of what for years had been our magic carpet.

This is another part of our love story that's difficult to talk about, so please bear with me. Between you and me, I'm not sure my memory is perfect. I can only tell you how I recall events. And I don't think it matters whether I get the dates in exact order. What does matter is that something malignant was about to steal into my relationship with Farrah, something that had never bedeviled us before: cheating. The dates are secondary. What did and did not happen and how we felt about it is primary. We let loose the jealousy genie, and once it was out of the bottle, we would both be condemned to live with its torment.

James Orr is directing *Man of the House*. Farrah introduces us. He's the kind of guy who has an unnecessarily firm handshake. He's not wearing a tie, and he's left the top three buttons of his shirt open. He's trying to prove something. I don't know what it is, but I'm neither impressed nor trusting. She's too comfortable around him. Though I tell myself I'm letting my imagination get the better of me, I can't help wondering if there's something going on between them. On the plane to New York, I feel sick.

For the next four months I throw myself into work on *Faithful*, grateful for the distraction. After Farrah wraps on *Man of the House*, she visits me on the set for a few days. While I'm still smoldering with suspicion, I keep my doubts about Farrah's fidelity to myself. I wish I could say that I held my tongue for practical reasons, such as it would have been unprofessional for me to engage in that kind of conversation with her when I was in the middle of making a movie. Truth is, I didn't say anything because to look her in the eye and ask her whether she was with James Orr would have made it real. The longer I avoided the question, the longer I could go on pretending it was only my imagination. Farrah sensed I was being icy but didn't try to thaw me. When I finally do muster the courage to confront her, she'll deny it. Though she would get involved with Orr later in 1997 after we break up, with disastrous consequences, she always insisted that nothing happened before that. There's a part of me that wants to believe her, and another that can't. It's only now that I'm able to put away my ego and appreciate just how extraordinary our relationship was, which is why looking back I have to make certain judgments, regardless of how painful. It's taken me all these years to realize there's no such thing as a perfect relationship, but true love, anointed by human frailty and nourished by forgiveness and acceptance, does exist. And Farrah and I had it. We just took a long time to realize it.

Farrah's visit to the set of *Faithful* is marred by resentments and insecurities on both sides. At first I can't understand why she keeps asking me if I have a thing for Cher. I'd known Cher for years. She has a house down the street in Malibu. She was one of Tatum's early adult friends and we've always had a nice rapport. But I've never been remotely attracted to the woman (not that she isn't appealing); indeed, there was never any chemistry for either of us. I find myself starting to wonder if Farrah's irrational concern about Cher is the by-product of a guilty conscience. I become convinced Farrah cheated on me. I envision her lying next to James Orr, sharing a private joke, laughing and cuddling in the way that I believed was mine alone. I start obsessing about Vancouver, replaying every detail in my head like video footage on a loop, the way she leaned into him when they spoke, the abrupt change in their body language

This photo was taken around 1950 when Farrah was three years old. You could see that legendary beauty in her even then.

My brother and I in our birthday best with Mom and Dad.

Above: Griffin, Farrah, and I in happier times, at the Pierre Hotel in New York for the premiere of Griffin's movie, *The Escape Artist.* This photo was taken in 1982.

Right: Patrick and I when he was a teen. The handsome kid has become a handsome man.

Yours truly with Farrah and my "ma" and "da." What I remember most about my parents is their wonderful marriage, how deeply they loved each other.

One of my favorite photos of Tatum and me. She was about ten here. I was in my early thirties.

Above:
Tatum and Griffin. Brother and sister remain close to this day. This shot would have been taken when they were middle-school age.

Left: My brood and I at Farrah's house on Antelo on my forty-second birthday. From left to right, Tatum, me, Griffin, and Patrick.

Adoring mom and baby in their pajamas.

Right: The proud grandfather Jimbo, his daughter Farrah, new grandson Redmond, and grandmother Pauline. This shot was taken in April 1985.

Below: Farrah, our son, and Tatum.

One of my favorite photos of the two sisters together.

My three sons—Patrick, Red, and Grif. This would have been
taken in the mid-eighties.

A typical gathering in Montauk, the farthest Hampton. From left to right, Steve Rubell, owner of the legendary Studio 54, designer Halston, me, the exquisite Ms. Minnelli, and her husband Marc Gero.

Above:
Farrah and I with agent Sue Mengers. This shot was taken in the early eighties. Sue was an extraordinary woman and a brilliant agent, and she will be missed by so many, me included.

Left: Farrah and I in the first bloom of our love. This would have been the early eighties.

These are a few examples of the notes Farrah left me almost daily. I've kept every one of them.

Darling R.O.,
I love you for being so sweet to me this weekend.
Good food, good fun, good sleep... opps!
I love you,
FF

A note FOR Ryan,
I had the best time. Thank you, thank you...... Call me — Sheddler won!!
I miss you already.
Love,
Farrah

R.O.,
I miss you already. Free me. Today is Ash Wednesday + beginning of Lent!
I love you madly
Farrah

Red and I at Farrah's funeral mass.

Shattered.

whenever I walked into the room, the furtive glances, the whispered exchanges. The boxer in me wanted to beat the tar out of this guy and reclaim my woman. Instead I buried my anger and pretended we could get past it, and Farrah became the great enabler, equally as determined not to deal with it. Neither of us played fair. Neither of us was capable of self-criticism. So we let it go. After she leaves, I reassure myself that everything will return to normal once the renovations on the little house are complete and we're back in familiar surroundings. Now, at seventy years old, I've come to understand that normal is the cuttlefish of illusions, that we each create our own normal that can change at will, and it is almost never what we expect.

By the end of 1994, we've moved out of the rental on Coldwater Canyon and have settled into the guesthouse on Antelo, splitting our time between there and the beach. Even in the stained light of loss, we could still pretend we were one of Hollywood's golden couples. When the paparazzi asked kindly, we'd pose. The invitations to awards ceremonies arrived. We stopped to sign autographs outside our favorite restaurants. And we were asked to make appearances at all the big charitable events and endorse a dizzying array of products. We did little or none of this. Though we always smiled for the cameras and at each other, behind closed doors we were living a different reality. We didn't trust each other anymore. James Orr may have been a reason, but he was not the cause. If Farrah did have an affair, it's time for me to take a hard look at how I may have been complicit. I don't want to fool myself. I want to make peace with the truth. I drove her away and neither one of us possessed the confidence to have that conversation that would have allowed us to make amends. These two lately discovered letters say it well.

MY DARLING RYAN,

You have given me so much and taught me so much that I could never repay you and you've shown me the best of what love can be. I will be eternally grateful that you touched my life and gave me Redmond. But your unhappiness has started to destroy all our dreams and I realize your dreams have changed. You deserve to be happy because when you are there is no one like you in the world. You must find that again and even though I don't want it be without me (this is so hard for me), I know it's coming. We will never be the same and I don't want to live in constant fear, and made to feel like I feel now. Unloved, depressed, with no hope in sight. My heart aches and I'm no good to anyone. The happiness has left my heart, for you were my heart.

FARRAH

This was clipped to it, apparently my response.

F.F.,

*Once upon a time I would have followed you
anywhere in the world, and usually did. I forgave
your cheating heart, although I cannot understand
your motives for such acts of disloyalty against
someone who loved you so much he broke with his
own kin. I'm not the man I was, I'm afraid, and
so it is easy to lose your temper with me and want
me out of your system. I'm sick at heart over the
silences, the locked doors, the stupidity that has
taken over our lives. True love begins and ends with
a mutual trust and instead all I've got is a misplaced
soul. My spirit for the game has been lost and until I
can find out what happened to my inner strength I'll
never be what you want or need. I was always true
blue when it came to you, just not to myself, it seems.
I'll try and not give up even though you have.
There was never a day I didn't love you.*

If we had an argument, we might kiss and make up, which is what we did after exchanging these letters, but underneath, resentment built. I wish I would have taken Farrah by the hand, sat her down, and forced us both to take responsibility for how we'd treated each other. It could have prevented a lot of heartache. And there would be much more in the coming months, and not just for Farrah and me, but for Tatum too.

By the new year, she and John have divorced, leaving a trail of tabloid scat in their wake. It had been coming for a while. But I don't need to get into all those details. My daughter has written two books on the subject. Speaking as her dad, the failure of her marriage was deeply disappointing. Though you know how I feel about John, I really did believe he'd be the anchor my daughter needed. Instead, she went overboard and soon found herself dragged under in a sea of drugs and alcohol. Next, Tatum would be embroiled in a bitter custody battle. John would eventually triumph. If Tatum's listening, she won't like hearing this, but I don't blame my former son-in-law for fighting for his kids the way he did. In fact, I respect him for it. No father wants to yank his children away from their mom. It's a gut-wrenching fight and everyone loses a part of her- or himself on the battle-field. I ought to know. I went after Joanna for custody of Tatum and Griffin, twice, for the same reason John had to duke it out with Tatum. I had no choice. At the time, my ex-wife was washing down half a bottle of barbiturates a day with vodka. And this was back in the early seventies when the courts favored the mother even if she was unfit. "Let's give her another chance," the judge said. To Joanna's credit, when she realized she was hopelessly addicted, she showed up on my doorstep in Malibu and handed me our kids, then checked into a hospital. Tatum was seven years old and Griffin was six. I can only imagine how hard that was for Joanna, and to this day, I don't know whether either of my children appreciates the courage that decision took. The rest of the story gets more complicated, with fundamental disagreement between my children and me over the specifics of how it unfolded. I can only say this: Joanna and I made some dreadful mistakes as parents, and I hope that one day my children will be able to forgive us, as they would want their own children to forgive them.

That was about forty years ago. My daughter inherited her mother's predilection for addiction but not her wisdom or compassion. And it was always either/or with Tatum. She was unfamiliar with subtlety. Innocent of nuance. Tatum is still tearing holes in her world and unfortunately her world at the moment is also mine. I promised to tell you what happened in New York. Brace yourself. I'll set the scene for you.

It's midafternoon exactly one week ago today. I'm sitting in the greenroom at CNN watching my daughter tape her interview with Piers Morgan. The "greenroom" is where talk show guests are parked until they go on camera. Some, like David Letterman's, are lavish, with soft leather couches, an elaborate buffet. and a fridge stocked with beverages; others, you're lucky if you can get a cup of water. At least this one has fresh hot coffee and bagels. I wish it had a dispenser of knockout drops alongside the cream and sugar. I can't believe what's coming out of my daughter's mouth. She's telling Piers that she first started experimenting with drugs at eleven years old. She knows that's not true! He's now inquiring if I supplied her with the drugs. "You'll have to ask him," she replies. Ask *him*? He doesn't need to ask me! Tatum, you and I both know the answer to that question is no! At this point, I'm hollering at the TV screen. A network page comes running in to ask if everything is all right. "Are you listening to this?" I say. "She's rewriting history! She hated drugs when she was little!" The page nods politely.

I turn my attention back to the show, trying to ignore the nagging question now hovering at the back of my mind: Could she actually have been doing drugs that young? Could I have been so clueless that I missed it? I remember after I got full custody, I put both Tatum and Griffin into a private school and she hated it there, started stealing and getting into trouble. I took her out of that school, and soon after we went into production on *Paper Moon*, where she had a tutor. No, I tell myself firmly. I may not have been the best father, certainly not a perfect one, but I would have known it if she was chewing Quaaludes at eleven. She probably thinks it looks better if her drug problem was a lifelong struggle rather than something that happened to her as an adult. I'm guessing, grasping, trying to come up with a reason why my daughter would misrepresent about something like this. Now my child is telling Piers to remember to speak up when he interviews me because I'm old and don't hear too well anymore. Well, young lady, I certainly heard that! Then, tossing back her hair, Tatum looks into the camera, smiles coquettishly, and adds, "I don't think my father can see too well anymore either." So I'm not only going deaf, I'm also going *blind*? I

stand up and begin shaking the television screen. The page
has now picked up the phone and is calling for backup. Okay,
maybe I'm exaggerating a little, but I want to flee. But then
I realize I've made this commitment and in fifteen minutes
I'll have to face Piers Morgan myself and answer questions
I'd rather not even hear. I ask Farrah to give me strength and
take several deep meditative breaths to calm down. By the
time the sound tech arrives to attach my mike, I feel confident and ready. Besides, I tell myself, it can't go any worse
than *Good Morning America*, the day before. At least this
interview is taped and I'm going on alone. *Good Morning
America* was live and Tatum and I were interviewed together.
And this time, I'm wearing comfortable clothing, a favorite
dark jacket over my lucky blue shirt, not that ridiculous suit
and tie they forced me to wear on ABC. Let me say that I'm
not now nor have I ever been a "morning person." I wore that
suit only because it was so early I was only half awake, without the wit to resist. When I saw the segment, I was mortified. I looked like a buffoon in that thing, not to mention that
my face was still puffy with sleep, and in my haste to be on
time, I'd failed to comb my hair. In the days of yore, you'd
never catch Cary Grant or Bill Holden with bags under their
eyes squinting into a camera in the wee hours, plugging their
latest project. They had too much dignity. And Tatum and
I were both so stiff and uncomfortable with each other, the
interviewer actually had to ask us on air to sit closer together.
This time, I reassure myself, I'll have more control.

Perhaps it was the shirt, which didn't seem to be lucky after all, that caused me to make mistakes with Piers Morgan. In my defense, the guy is so good at what he does he had me feeling as if we were chatting over tea and scones. And all I wanted to do was tell my side of the story. Instead, I ended up generating nearly a week's worth of tawdry headlines because of one comment that didn't come out the way I meant it. Tatum has barely spoken to me since. There are certain things you might believe or speculate about that you shouldn't mention in polite company, let alone on national television. I know a movie executive who actually believes in UFOs. He has a huge telescope and he and his young son scan the skies a couple of times a month looking for a mother ship. But he's got the sense not to talk about it when there are journalists around. I should have learned from his example. I essentially accused the O'Neal family of accelerating Farrah's premature death. I'm not the only one who thinks there's a link between illness and stress. But there's not a lot of scientific evidence to support that belief. It was a foolhardy attempt to be honest. I'm like the guy who's surprised to discover that Walmart sells health insurance. I shouldn't be. That's what Walmart does. They sell everything. So why am I surprised that the scandal sheets pounced on my thoughtless remarks?

But enough of that. We were talking about 1995. Being an actor, I sometimes think about my life as if it were a script. It gives me perspective. And if Farrah and Ryan were

fictional characters in a made-for-TV movie about that year
and I was writing the screenplay, these would be some of my
production notes.

FARRAH:

We meet a frustrated, angry woman whose once
delicate features are tight and pinched.
There are new lines on her face and she has
circles under her eyes. She feels unappreci-
ated by Ryan, taken for granted. She's the
one who has to do everything: be the disci-
plinarian for their son, Redmond; run two
households; manage the day-to-day minutia of
their lives while Ryan wallows in self-pity,
his moods and outbursts kidnapping the joy
their family once knew. There are no boundaries. And she's exhausted being made responsible for his feelings as well as her own.
Enter Griffin, the prodigal son, who invites
his younger half brother into his world. A
montage of images: a strung-out thirty-year-
old Griffin, roach clip dangling from his key
chain, a packet of Easy Rider rolling papers
peeking out from his pocket, jamming on
drums with his adoring ten-year-old brother;
a teary-eyed Redmond running after Griffin
and his buddies, begging to be taken along as

they're pulling out of the driveway. A dream sequence: an anxious Farrah, sitting alone in a theater watching her worst fear unfolding: Redmond turning his life over to Griffin. She keeps attempting to climb onto the stage and insinuate herself into the play so she can change the ending. A blond hulk keeps pushing her back. A series of shots depicting Farrah with Redmond: mother and son tearing down the driveway on skateboards; an art class where she and Redmond are sitting side by side, he's clasping a paintbrush and she's guiding his hand across the canvas. Late at night, a shot of the living room, a disengaged Ryan is draped across the couch with his book, then cut to the basement, where we see Griffin, half stoned and listening to a Grateful Dead album with Redmond asleep in his lap. Cut to the downstairs hallway, where we hear Farrah weeping from the other side of the closed bathroom door.

RYAN:

He's sick and tired of Farrah's constant anger and can't understand why no matter how hard he tries, he can't please her or dilute the disappointment he sometimes sees in her eyes

when she looks at him. He tells himself that
she's the one who should be trying to please
him, that it wasn't he who sought refuge in
the arms of another. His resentment builds.
Reenter Griffin, whom Ryan will defend
against an indignant Farrah, not realizing
that before the decade is over, Redmond will
follow his big brother down the rabbit hole.
Scene opens with the exterior of Ryan's gym,
then cut to Ryan on the treadmill. His shirt
is soaked with sweat and he's out of breath,
yet he keeps pushing himself. A close-up of
his face. He's aged since we saw him last.
There are visible signs of strain around the
eyes and mouth. He's unshaved. The camera
illustrates his dilemma. We see images of a
trembling Redmond begging Ryan to make Mommy
stop yelling all the time; Farrah grabbing
another pack of antibiotics from the stash in
her medicine cabinet and popping them like
vitamins; a series of quick scenes depicting a
parade of dubious New Age healers, with their
tie-dyed sacks of potions and herbs slung
across their shoulders, coming in and out of
the house; Ryan lying on the couch pretending
to be reading to avoid another argument; Ryan
hesitating by the bathroom door, listening to

Farrah's tears, longing to comfort her; he's
about to knock on the door, hesitates, then
retreats once again to the couch.

But we weren't fictional characters. We were two very
real, very human people who were disillusioned with each
other. I started withdrawing emotionally not because I had
stopped loving Farrah; I still adored her but it had become a
matter of self-preservation. Everything set her off. If someone forgot to take a telephone message, she'd rage. If you dis-
agreed with her about a quiz show question, she'd stomp out
of the room. And what you have to realize is that this wasn't
like Farrah. She was always spirited, but this was something
new. It was as if an evil stranger had reached inside and
cranked up her anger generator. I remember I had bought
Redmond a painting of his favorite baseball player, Ernie
Banks, and hadn't yet gotten around to hanging it. Farrah
noticed it leaning on the dresser and started a tirade, and
by the time her energy was spent, she had attacked my kids,
my ex-wife's lifestyle, and my politics. It was as if the painting had ignited a string of ancient fights and offenses that
had to play itself out for her to be able to breathe again. It
got to the point where I started escaping to the beach house
while Farrah sought refuge in her art, sculpting and draw-
ing. We became skilled at seeking shelter from each other.
The one who suffered most was Redmond, who couldn't escape either of us. No wonder he was susceptible to Griffin's

example. Looking back now, I believe that our not having married exerted a greater influence on our little family than we realized. We were both so cavalier about the idea of marriage, and when we finally decided we wanted to do it, had to do it, by then fate had other plans. But would we have tried harder if we hadn't each owned separate homes, if we were forced to adhere to the conventions of marriage, a man and wife living together under one roof? Would our script have been written differently?

By the end of 1995, I had convinced myself that Farrah's unsettling state of mind was due to menopause. I figured in six months it would pass. I can see you shaking your head. I'm not of the generation that talks about these things. Most of what I knew about "the change" came from Edith and Archie Bunker in that famous episode from *All in the Family*. And by the end of the third commercial Edith's hormones are fine. For the record, I did ask my mom about it too. She said I shouldn't worry, that Farrah would be back to herself shortly. She wasn't.

As winter surrendered to spring, I, too, felt like giving up. For her forty-eighth birthday, Farrah had posed seminude for a *Playboy* spread, and they put her on the cover. It was an international sensation. I remember holding the issue in my hands, thinking to myself, "Look at you. You have everything: a man who loves you, a beautiful son, the world at attention; so what's wrong? Why can't you crawl out of this dark place you're in before you drag us both down?" Men can occasionally be stupid. Since *Good Sports*, her bouts of poor health were suspiciously regular—sinus infections, colds—but now, instead of letting her body heal on its own, she'd pump herself full of antibiotics. It was her drug of choice, her security blanket. I can only imagine what they did to her immune system. I watched the woman I love disarm her body's natural ability to fight off diseases. Oh, I'd warn her that taking a Z-Pak for her head cold wasn't either smart or effective. I tried to explain that it's like the boy who cried wolf. Take the antibiotics when you don't need them, I'd tell her, and they won't work when you do need them. But she wouldn't listen.

She was leaning on anything available to give her strength and it wasn't working. Was it possible that all those years with me and my kids had stripped her of her fortitude, and then when the day came that she needed to draw upon her reserve, there was nothing left? I asked one of the New Age gurus who had come to my house a few times, Dr. Mumbo Jumbo, why he was treating her. He said, "To cleanse the lining of her soul." How could Farrah have been that desperate and lost? How could I have been so self-involved that I didn't see it? Don't answer. I already know what you're going to say and you're right. Where was I during all this? Running off to the gym for hours each day, immersing myself in racquetball, squash, handball, tennis, boxing, and weight training, becoming obsessive about staying fit. Even after multiple operations on my knees, I still couldn't stop pushing myself. I was becoming neurotic, and writing about this now, I realize it wasn't much different from Farrah's addiction to antibiotics or her reliance on witch doctors. We were both trying to harness our bodies because our lives felt so pointless. I was exhausting myself to achieve what passed for a peaceful state of mind. And I was running from the things that were haunting me: my failures as a parent, the career I should have had but didn't. And all the while Farrah was melting. We both missed it happening in each other, like two tops spinning so fast, all we could see was a blur.

Then my father died.

CHAPTER SEVEN

FALLING APART
TOGETHER

It doesn't matter how old you are when you lose a parent. The grief never entirely recedes. I loved my father deeply and we had a strong, honest relationship. Born and raised in North Carolina, he was a gentleman, a kind and decent man. It's probably one of the reasons why he didn't achieve success befitting his accomplishments. This was a subject we never talked about; it was just something I sensed as a kid. My dad's ambition was eclipsed by his values; he couldn't step on others no matter what the reason, and he got shortchanged in this town because of it. He was never bitter about it. Hollywood, like Washington politics, can steal your soul. You enter the arena a young idealist and begin moving up the ladder, one rung at a time, each one slippery with ruthlessness and cynicism, and by the time you reach the top, you wonder why you barely recognize yourself. My dad never let this place change him.

He migrated here fresh out of college, which is where he was given the nickname Blackie. His first name was Charles. He initially came to Hollywood for the same reason thousands of other hopefuls did: to become an actor. He joined an acting troupe, which is where he met my mom, Patricia.

After publishing a short story in *Esquire*, he decided to forgo performing and concentrate on writing. Over the next three decades he would write for both film and television. He wrote the screenplays for many low-budget B movies that would become cult classics, such as *The Seventh Victim* and *Cry of the Werewolf*, both produced by RKO Pictures' head of horror Val Lewton, an irreverent genius whose work influenced filmmakers from Hitchcock to Scorsese.

I remember my dad bringing me on set when I was growing up. Back in those days some of the biggest stars from the golden era were reduced to B movies later in their careers. I got to meet many of them: Ethel Barrymore, Errol Flynn, Deanna Durbin, Donald O'Connor, all of whom starred in movies that my dad wrote. That early experience, witnessing how in Hollywood even the greats were relegated to the sidelines once they'd outlived their glory, stayed with me. I'm still haunted by some of those faces, how sad and empty they looked.

I have many wonderful memories with my dad. One of his favorite jobs was writing for the popular television series *The Untouchables*, starring Robert Stack. He once put me in an episode. He incorporated my mom into a couple of episodes too. Dad also did a lot of work in Europe. When I was in high school, our family moved to Germany, where he was writing broadcasts for Radio Free Europe. During that period I landed my first job, as a stand-in/stunt man for an American television series shooting in Germany:

Tales of the Vikings. It was magical, and to my dad's credit, he never discouraged me from becoming an actor. When we returned to the States, I accepted every role offered and eventually built my way up to *Peyton Place,* a hugely popular nighttime soap opera that launched my career and introduced America to a brilliant young talent, Mia Farrow. Remind me to tell you later the story about how she met Frank Sinatra. But back to my parents . . . My dad didn't start slowing down until his late eighties, when his memory began to dim. I recognized he was declining after I started

Yours truly in glorious youth.

noticing scratches and dents on the Cadillac I'd bought him. He was proud of that car, so I knew something was wrong when he couldn't understand how it had been damaged. Dad played Big Ten football at the University of Iowa, where he was an honorable mention all-American. In those days they wore leather helmets. It's a miracle his memory stayed sharp until he was nearly ninety.

I credit my mother for my father's good health and longevity. She lived another ten years after my dad passed in 1996. She was his most ardent admirer and supporter. She proofread all of his work, and I

can still hear their exchanges, her offering her critique on a
particular scene and his spirited response to her usually apt
assessments. They were the consummate team, maybe because they adored each other. And what a couple they made,
my mom with her petite frame, auburn hair, and blue eyes,
and my dad, tall and broad shouldered, with his masculine
good looks. He was one of those men who believed a woman
should be treated like a lady. He would always open the car
door for my mother, pull out her chair, wait patiently for her
to "put on her face" for the evening, and then beam when
he'd see her coming down the stairs.

Every family has its legends, and we have ours. I've
researched it and can't find any references, but this is the
story my mother told me: My mom's maiden name was
O'Callaghan. Her mother was born in Russia; her father,
my maternal grandfather, was from Ireland. He was a tinker
and supposedly invented the electric heater alleged to have
started the Seattle fire of 1910. Apparently, my grandfather
needed to make a hasty retreat from Seattle to avoid authori-
ties who wanted to arrest him for toasting the town, and so
he packed up my grandmother and my mom and they de-
camped to Toronto, where my mom lived most of her early
years. I don't know if any of this is true, but isn't it a grand
story?

Though my mom would take on bit parts occasionally,
she was a self-selected wife and mother, though she had a
small but memorable role in *Rosemary's Baby*. She was our

anchor and our nurturer. I also have a younger brother, Kevin. He's struggled with health issues most of his life. He suffered two terrible brain aneurysms when he was young, which have limited his activity. He was an amateur boxer like me, not the best exercise for someone who has a fragile brain.

When I look back on my youth, I can't help but wonder how someone raised in a stable and loving environment could have ended up making such a mess of his own family life. I suspect my parents must have had moments when they asked themselves, "Did we go wrong somewhere?" My mistakes as a husband and father are mine and I take responsibility for the painful parts of my life as well as the joyful ones. Our parents may set the stage, but we're the ones who determine what our characters will do as our lives are

My brother Kevin and I in our prime.

played out. It's what Tatum struggles with daily. My parents instilled in me a sense of hope and optimism, the instinct to see the best in others, and it's on me, not them, that my expectations were unrealistic. At first I was too young. By the time I began to figure it out, I'd been married and divorced twice, was still in my late twenties, and had three children. The trail I was on got twisted and I couldn't straighten it out. The sad irony is that there's a fallout from growing up in a happy home. To this day I carry with me some of the belief that all will end well just because it should. It was my coping mechanism when I found out Tatum had become addicted to heroin and was entering her third stint in rehab. Maybe not the best response I could have had, but when a daughter has banished you, what choice is left? Being a Pollyanna was better than losing all hope.

This feckless sense of human nature also colored my time with Farrah. I kept praying everything would be all right between us, but by the end of 1996, our problems had escalated. Farrah and I were also guilty of a mistake many couples make: we both expected our mutual love for Redmond would be enough to get us through anything. We were relying on him to be our savior, and no child should ever have to carry that burden. We weren't unlike the couple who get pregnant thinking a baby will fix whatever is broken in their marriage. It never works, and it didn't for us either. Redmond's grades started slipping again, his attitude worsened, and he turned to—you guessed it—Griffin. I loved all three of my sons and desperately wanted to believe that Griffin's efforts to change his ways were genuine despite masses of evidence to the contrary. I thought that if I believed in him hard enough, eventually he'd believe in himself. Farrah knew better. I wish I'd listened to her, but at the time I had on glasses with a rose tint. I don't anymore. A fireplace poker shattered them, but I'm getting ahead of myself. We were discussing the end of 1996. Our little family was imploding and Farrah and I sensed it, but we had grown so accustomed to evading the obvious that only shock or tragedy could jolt us out of our foolishness. We would be hit with both. A series of seemingly innocuous events would precipitate their arrival.

We're nearing Christmas. I'm in production for a new comedy, *Burn Hollywood Burn.* The screenwriter is Joe Eszterhas, whose list of box office successes includes *Basic Instinct* and *The Jagged Edge,* and Arthur Hiller is directing it. He was the director on *Love Story,* and to be back on the Paramount lot, working with him after twenty-five years, is a homecoming. Every morning I wake up full of energy, eager to begin the day. I haven't felt this good about a role in a long time. The excitement on set is terrific and everyone from cast to crew is spot on their game. I want to stand on the hood of my car and shout, "I'm back!" There would be some serious chemistry off set too, but I'll get to that in a minute. Making this job even sweeter is that I don't have to be on location. The entire film is being shot down the street from my beach house, where, sadly, I've been spending most nights alone. At this point, Farrah and I are barely living together. Our relationship has reached its nadir.

> **JOURNAL ENTRY, DECEMBER 20, 1996**
> My hand is shaking as I write this. She turned on me again. She's coming unhinged before my very eyes, obsessing about a video camera at the beach house, insisting I left it there. I know for a fact it's somewhere here in her house. Then, she's telling me that I'm dirt. I guess I am for taking it from her. I begin to seethe and the next thing I hear is myself hollering back at her for always blaming me for whatever goes wrong.

When I read these journal entries, I cringe. We had so much together, and we let it sour over everything and nothing. Who cares about a video camera? If she was having a bad day and had it in her head that I left the camera at the beach house, why did I have to contradict her? Why not just say okay, I'll look for it, and if we can't find it, I'll buy a new one? I know what you've concluded and you're right. If it wasn't the video camera, it would have been something else. The two of us together had become a steaming volcano. There was so much hostility bubbling beneath the surface of our relationship that these small eruptions were our only means of releasing the pressure. Our only safe place was sex. But soon even that, the one aspect of our love for each other that was never used to hurt or humiliate, would be poisoned. And in order to breathe, we'd both seek a fresh source of air. Ironically, I'd find mine on the set of *Burn Hollywood Burn,* but it would be several months before I'd inhale. Her name was Leslie, an actress twenty-five years my junior who was costarring in the film. A graduate of Barnard, she was a smart girl, attractive and sweet, a decent, God-fearing Episcopalian from a small town in Minnesota who didn't have the complexities and complications that Farrah did. Her life was much simpler. I didn't pursue Leslie nor she me. It unfolded gradually. At first I thought of her as refreshing youth, innocent without being naive, kind without being fawning. Then one morning I realized that the first two things I'd look for on the set were my cup of coffee and her smiling face.

When I wasn't filming, I was helping Farrah with a video project for *Playboy.* The editors were so impressed by the sales numbers from her cover spread that they asked if she'd do a second one. When she agreed, they suggested an accompanying video to commemorate her fiftieth birthday. She came up with the concept and it was brilliant. By this time she was serious about developing her talents as a sculptor and painter. While audiences may remember Farrah as an actress, she was also an artist. She had always wanted to try body art, in which she would cover herself with paint and use her torso as the brush painting the canvas. Playboy loved the concept so I began working with her on the production of the video. It was an arduous but exhilarating process. Despite the personal tension, she still relied upon my judgment when it came to her career. As disenchanted as we had become with each other, I couldn't bear not to play that role in her life, and after *Good Sports,* I didn't have confidence that she'd want or need me, so I was grateful to be asked.

Over Christmas, Farrah finds another cyst on her breast. Over the years, she'd had several removed, all of which were benign, but this one is in a more troublesome spot and causing acute pain. Though it turns out to be benign like the others, I was uneasy during her surgery, never imagining that it was fate's version of a dress rehearsal. As we toasted the new year in 1997, I believed Farrah was fine and so resented the medical intrusion on our holidays because during the two weeks she was home recuperating, she was ornerier than ever. What with menopause, which had now been going on far longer than dear old mother had promised me, Farrah's swiftly approaching dreaded birthday, and Griffin and Redmond's growing attachment to each other, I should have smelled the sulfur. Krakatoa à la Fawcett-O'Neal was getting ready to erupt.

JOURNAL ENTRY, JANUARY 5, 1997

I fled from her last night, turned off my light, and lost myself in sleep. Farrah read my diary, a capital crime to some but not to me. She found something that infuriated her. God knows what. She tried to kick me in the groin, the most hated part of me. This with a breast full of stitches in her. I stagger off to bed and leave her throwing Christmas ornaments at my door. The disdain we feel for each other has come to the point of violence. Why doesn't she love me anymore?

I want to stop here for a moment and say something. Yes, it's true. Farrah and I did occasionally get physical with each other when we fought. Neither of us possessed the emotional discipline to say wait a minute, this isn't normal, we need help. But it wasn't the way the journalists depicted it. You have to remember that I'm a trained boxer. I sparred with the world champion Joe Frazier, and if someone is coming at me with fists flailing or feet pointed at my family jewels, my instinct is to block the blows, which is what I did with Farrah. Back then there was no YouTube, but if there had been and someone had shot footage of our skirmishes, it would have generated millions of hits not because of the violence but for the slapstick dance. I'm not trying to make light of Farrah's and my tussles with each other; still, most of the time, I found her outbursts oddly endearing because they were so ludicrous, so childlike. They were also courting serious injury. I should have paid more attention to the signs that something was amiss, that something was building, growing, and might one day explode. It had been percolating for years. But I was bedazzled. I loved everything about her, even her infantile display of temper, which I associated with her being fiery and passionate. By 1997, her conduct

unbecoming was more likely to ignite anger than bemuse-
ment, and in defending myself I didn't see my behavior as
aberrant. Most men of my generation would have reacted
the same way. That doesn't make it right.

But there was so much not right during this period that
how we fought was simply one more obstacle to finding our
way back to each other. Another, which I'm only beginning
to recognize now, is that Farrah and I took most everything
too personally. We may have seemed as confident as Ken
and Barbie, but underneath, we were unsure of ourselves.
If she was in a bad mood because of a tense moment on set
or a dispiriting article, and she snapped at me, I didn't have
the wit to stand back and say, "She's not really angry with
me, it's that cretin of a reporter from the *National Enquirer*."
Farrah was the same way. She interpreted a lot of my bad
behavior personally too, when in reality, most of the time,
it wasn't her I was lashing out at, it was my kids, the world,
Hollywood, my agent, you name it. I'm a moody guy, as are
many actors. I've walked out of the middle of my own dinner parties. It doesn't even require a trigger.

Our anger was misplaced. Farrah and I should have directed it toward the shared enemy lurking outside our front
door, the same one I saw reflected in all those tired smiles
on my dad's low-budget movie sets: aging in an industry
that genuflects before the altar of youth. The downward
spiral in many show business careers has more to do with
the year you were born than with your talent. Even when

your expiration date arrives, you keep on going, hoping no one will look too closely at that number stamped on your forehead. Farrah and I both feared it. We never discussed it, probably for the same reason we didn't talk about James Orr. We wanted to keep pretending it wasn't real. But the truth of our business is that the older you become, the more meager your opportunities for work. When you're starting out and going on auditions, you have a future to look forward to; when you get to be our age, it's the reverse, and there's a terrible reluctance to admit the transition. Look at what I'm doing now in my dotage: cable television. At least Tatum didn't force me to try out for the reality show. And Arthur Hiller would never have directed *Burn Hollywood Burn*, a comedy with a substandard budget and (sorry Joe) a controlling screenwriter/producer, if he were still in his prime. And speaking of dramatic irony. The movie is about a director who ends up hating his film so much that he steals the reels to prevent it from being released. In real life, Hiller so disliked the final cut of *Burn Hollywood Burn* that he insisted on having his good name removed from the credits. I was an actor. I didn't have that option. What was I supposed to do, have special effects black out my face?

I had passed the half-century mark by 1997, and while it haunted me in quiet moments, I had survived that initial wave of psychological nausea. Farrah hadn't. Weeks away from her fiftieth birthday, she was in a panic, the all-American girl now tormented by the same beauty that catapulted her to fame and that she could see was fading. Farrah was notorious for being tardy, but at this point in her life, it had gotten perverse. She would spend hours in the bathroom, staring at her face in the mirror. Once, early in our relationship, we were late for a dinner with the president of the United States and Nancy Reagan because I couldn't convince Farrah that she really did look fine. Over the succeeding years it got worse. I watched her slowly being consumed by insecurity, but I couldn't fully appreciate her anxiety. I would tell her, "You're beautiful, what are you worried about?" And to me she *was* beautiful, still exquisite. But instead of being patient with her fears and reassuring her, I felt offended that my word wasn't good enough.

As the clock ticked, so did the time bomb. One moment Farrah and I are making love, and I'm reading to her, and then she's whipping up a batch of chili con carne just the way I like it; the next, she's dictating a press release to her publicist announcing our breakup. Some days we'd argue by voice mail, and there would be a dozen incoherent messages on both machines. There were nights as I lay in bed listening to the surf while drifting off to sleep I ached to have her in my arms and would keep telling myself I could learn to adjust to the fractious tone that had come to define our time together. On some of those nights, I would pick up the phone, start to dial, and then stop myself. Was it fear or survival? I'm not sure. What I do know is that I couldn't bear the thought of leaving her any more than I could imagine our staying together. If I was in hell, Farrah was in purgatory. I had to breathe or I would have suffocated. So I finally inhaled the cool fresh air of Leslie. I wouldn't have succumbed if I could have seen into the future. I weakened. I didn't turn to anyone for advice. The one person I would have talked to about this was Blackie, and he was gone. He would have told me to stick it out with Farrah, to fight harder to save what we had. By Farrah's fiftieth birthday, I was torn between the girl who was helping me to catch my breath, and the only woman who was ever able to steal my heart. The day of her birthday, she didn't want a party. She had lunch with a few of her girlfriends, and that was it. Then she came to the beach house. We made love like the old days. It was magical, out of the pages of a fairytale. Come morning, the spell was broken, and soon both the princess and the prince were again wandering aimlessly, trying to find their way from once upon a time to they lived happily ever after.

Two weeks later, Farrah and I are where we were before, at each other's throats, then in each other's arms, then at each other's throats again. The difference now is that I can't rationalize it anymore and neither can she. At her request, I'm boxing her things at the beach house and arranging to have them moved to her place on Antelo. But disentangling ourselves from the cord of unresolved emotion won't prove as easy as packing boxes. Each night when I get home, I drop my keys on the table, pour a glass of wine, walk over to the phone, and stare at the blinking red light on my answering machine, tensing as I push the button to hear my messages. I suspect Farrah was engaged in the same sad exercise at her house. Voice messaging had now become our intermediary. A cold, metal contraption, that's where we vented our disappointment with each other. It became our catch-all, be-all, end-all, chicken-shit way of dealing with our troubles. I remember one night when she called late. I saw her number on my caller ID. I hesitated for a moment before answering, expecting another tirade. Her voice was soft, almost timid. She asked if I'd stay on the line with her while she said her prayers. Later I wept.

By now all the drama in our life was heartbreaking. I was at the beach house and had been inhaling and appreciating Leslie's aroma much the way one might a fine glass of wine. I knew there was something delicious there. I was ready to take a sip. Farrah calls and says she wants to come down to the beach.

"It's eleven o'clock," I say. "It's too late. Let's meet tomorrow."

"I want to come now."

"No, Farrah."

Leslie's listening. "Are you one hundred percent sure she's not going to come over?" she asks.

"Absolutely," I answer. "Farrah has her pride."

Truthfully, I was only 80 percent sure, but I figured the odds were with me, and I had locked the door just to be sure. At two in the morning I hear someone coming up the stairs and I gulp. In my groggy state, I briefly consider scaling down the terrace out to the beach and making a run for it, but then I remember my bad knee. I lean over and frantically begin whispering to Leslie, "Get up! get up!"

Farrah walks in.

Leslie and I are naked in bed.

Farrah must have let herself into the garage and gotten the house key out of my car.

Leslie pulls the covers over her head. I jump out of bed and pull on my shorts, putting both legs in one hole. Farrah is furiously yanking at the covers to get to Leslie, and I'm bouncing around mostly nude, sputtering inanities such as "This isn't what you think." By now Farrah has practically stripped the bed and is giving Leslie this withering, Bette Davis stare.

"What's your name," Farrah demands.

When Leslie doesn't answer, Farrah utters a warning, turns on her heel, and leaves, collecting photos and other things on her way out, personal items, including one of our beloved cherubs. I stumble down the stairs after her, trying to explain. I feel terrible and embarrassed for her, and I want to comfort her. I tell Farrah that Leslie isn't some girl I just picked up, that this is a woman I genuinely care about. I know, I know, not the smartest thing to say under the circumstances, but this had never happened to me before. In the eighteen years we'd been together, I'd never cheated on Farrah, not once. Now the boundaries of our relationship were blurred. We were living separate lives, and I wanted Farrah to know that I wouldn't just hop into bed with anyone. It would have to be with someone important, that I would never dishonor all that we had once shared by having casual sex with strangers. Farrah looks crestfallen, depleted of energy or caring. I thought I was saying all the right things but then realize what she must have been hearing, that I'd replaced her with a younger woman. That wasn't the case. Farrah had simply become too exhausting. I needed a breather. Leslie took care of me the way I once took care of Farrah, and it was great to be on the receiving end of gentle affection again. She was my nurse, my friend, and my confidante. I wanted her respect, and I measured the choices I made by what she would think of me. But the longer Leslie and I were together, the less hope she had in a future for us. Rather than our relationship strengthening over time, our connection would weaken because Farrah still inhabited her own room in my head.

Leslie and I would be together for four years. That relationship would be the most peaceful of my adult life. It would show me that I was capable of a mature, reciprocal relationship in which two people treat each other with respect and understanding. Leslie and I were, dare I say it, a normal, healthy couple. We never had fights because she insisted on talking things out. Though I admit I wasn't always the best student, she taught me by example the benefits of mutually engaging conversation. Most people assumed that I was beguiled by her youth. It was a lovely bonus, but not the prize. She possessed a wisdom, a sanguinity, and after a while both began to rub off on me and I started to like myself again. I began to remember how good it felt to be kind and generous and have it appreciated. Farrah saw all this too and was tortured. From the moment she discovered Leslie and me together that night at the beach, she slowly became rueful. I wouldn't understand just how much until recently when I made a disturbing discovery in one of my journals. That's all to come. Let me continue with the autumn of our discontent.

It didn't take long for the press to swoop down on the three of us. They were unrelenting. They staked out Farrah like a bail bondsman waiting for a fugitive. Photographers surrounded the house in Malibu. They tried to catch me going in and out of my gym, and they hounded Leslie. The poor girl was portrayed as the "red-headed floozy who stole Farrah's man," a Los Angeles Lolita. This was a small-town girl who wasn't used to being sullied. It was hard on her. That whole year is a blur to me now. Perhaps it's my mind's way of protecting itself. Here are the highlights, not necessarily in proper order.

Patrick and actress Rebecca DeMornay, who had been dating for a while, have their first child. They'll have another daughter in 2001. I establish trust funds for both, as I had previously for Griffin's children. Rebecca doesn't say a word to me.

Farrah's cast opposite Robert Duvall in *The Apostle*. She owns the part. I help her rehearse. Tracy and Hepburn couldn't have worked together as successfully in the wake of what she and I had just been through. That made it even harder. We could walk away, but we couldn't let go . . .

JOURNAL ENTRY, FEBRUARY 24, 1997
I saw Farrah at the gym today. It was our first meeting since it happened. She was wonderful and beautiful both. We cried together and I held her head. She asked if she could keep the ProGym shirt I was wearing, so sweet, she said, was the smell.

Nothing about Farrah and me seemed to have clarity. We couldn't even break up properly. I remember when Redmond fell on his skateboard and got a nasty scrape on his arm. He was still wearing the Band-Aid a week later, and it had become soiled and ragged, half of it dangling. He'd peel at it slowly, painfully, wincing from the sting of the adhesive tearing at the fine hairs on his skin. So one morning, I reached over and yanked it off. "See, that didn't even hurt," I said. He gave me a dirty look, and then admitted that my method was better than trying to remove it a millimeter at a time. That's what my relationship with Farrah felt like at this point, like a Band-Aid hanging from a wound, with each of us waiting for the other to pull it off. Instead, like Redmond, we both picked at it reluctantly, with not-so-gentle results. And then there was the infamous appearance on the *Late Show with David Letterman*. I didn't think it was so bad. I knew what she was trying to do. Her spread in *Playboy* magazine, the one for which we'd done the video, was coming out and she was attempting to play the part of a ditsy bunny, thinking it would be a clever way to promote the magazine. She called me that night in tears, saying that after the taping she was in the bathroom and overheard a group of women making vicious comments. "They thought I was on drugs," she said. I told her, "You're a fox, you're not a bunny, just let the photos speak for themselves and don't feel you have to be anyone other than yourself in these interviews." That stopped her tears but not the assault. Several months later the infamy was repeated, this time by the *Star*.

Here's an excerpt:

The Star, November 25, 1997
Wacky Farrah Fawcett is at it again . . . The Playboy pinup stunned onlookers when they saw her drive up to her ex-lover Ryan O'Neal's gym in a new Jaguar—only to sit in the front seat fiddling with her hair and touching up her makeup in the rearview mirror for more than an hour! "Finally a guy and a girl, they looked like they might be trainers, came out and

walked up to the car and started talking to her," says
a witness. Farrah went into the Pro-Gym, in Brentwood, Calif., came out, went back in, and came out
wearing a white tank top.

"She was looking around a lot. I don't know
what she was looking for. She was wiping her nose
a lot. Then she crossed the street, looking back and
forth, and picking her nose the whole time." Fawcett
raised eyebrows last June by acting very spaced out
on the Letterman show, and rumors of drug use and
emotional problems after her break from O'Neal
have plagued her.

We were supposed to meet about something to do with
Redmond's education. It was one of the few times that she
showed up on time and I was seriously late. It was discon-
certing. She'd thought I'd been in an accident. And who was
this so-called witness from the *Star*? Why is it these witnesses never have names?

I was surprised by the cruel attack on her from the
press and by the fact that they'd left me alone. It probably
indicated a shift in our relative status. For the first time, the
tabloids started saying that it wasn't Ryan who was crazy,
it was Farrah. I had always been the aberrant one. Now
the press had turned around and made her the loon, and
she didn't deserve it. Without each other, we had both become unmoored, but I had found a safe harbor with Leslie,

whereas Farrah was at the mercy of the cold wind. She was with other men now, and she'd only had a couple of men in her life. She didn't have experience and she made serious mistakes, the worst of which was getting involved with James Orr again. By 1998, he'll ask her to marry him. She'll refuse. So he'll beat her brutally, for which he will later be convicted and sentenced.

Other lowlights from 1997:

Tatum has become a certified junkie, and her poor troubled mother dies of lung cancer.

It wasn't a very good year.

CHAPTER EIGHT

DISCOVERIES

J ust as I began working on this book, I appeared on *Oprah* to commemorate the fortieth anniversary of *Love Story*. The highlight was spending some time with my co-star, the always-exquisite Ali MacGraw. I'd almost forgotten how wise and kind and generous she is. After the taping, we talked of Farrah, and I soon discovered that in some ways she understood the woman I'd spent thirty years with better than I did. So many people still retain this image of Farrah Fawcett as the ingenue pinup girl in a red bathing suit, and she was that, but as Ali reminisced, and I paraphrase here, "When they talk about people having the soul of an artist, that's usually an exaggeration but it was true with Farrah. Everything about her was genuine." But I knew there were doubts inside her too, serious doubts that our breakup would magnify. I've lately thought about why Farrah was able to retain her popular appeal over the decades while mine skidded south—reasons other than displays of my limping imitation of a parent. Girls and women could embrace her look and her style while not becoming jealous or threatened as they were by, say, Marilyn Monroe. Farrah was the embodiment of the all-American beauty. That boys and men responded to her sexually is a given, but they also sensed she'd make a great sister. My audience was primarily women. Male moviegoers don't much care for good-looking, careless young men. And neither my appearance nor my character improved over time. I was as cute to women as my friend Bill Holden at twenty but not as handsome and responsible at thirty or as distinguished and successful at fifty. That's a reason why I was vulnerable to Leslie: she adored me and I needed the affirmation.

Turns out I also still needed Farrah. Despite my deepening relationship with Leslie, I couldn't detach from Farrah, nor could she from me. I remember an occasion during this period when I accepted an invitation to Alana Stewart's house, knowing Farrah would be there. Alana Stewart, exwife of George Hamilton and Rod Stewart, was one of Farrah's closest friends and this was an impromptu dinner party. A few of the other people Alana was able to round up at the last minute were both her exes, George sporting his usual tan and Rod sporting his new wife. Also on hand were Jeff Goldblum, who always wanted to play Trivial Pursuit; Cheryl Tiegs, who looks as good in person as she does on the cover of *Vogue;* Michelle Phillips, without John or Mackenzie; Jackie Collins, whose conversation is as witty and entertaining as her juicy novels; and Suzanne Somers, who spent the evening talking with Dominick Dunne and producer Suzanne de Passe. As usual, I didn't take Leslie. Too much history with this crowd, and she never felt comfortable being around people who were a part of my life with Farrah. That night Farrah was in good spirits. I had to remind myself that we weren't a couple anymore. By the end of the evening, we were aching for a few moments alone together so we got into her car, drove a block, and parked. We talked for almost two hours, laughing and reminiscing. I kissed her goodnight—more than once. She was a beautiful kisser, her mouth tasted like vanilla mint. On the way back to get my car, we held hands. I resisted the urge to whistle.

As I drove home to the beach and Leslie, I felt both ex-hilarated and guilty, like a teenager out past curfew, but that was the magic of Farrah and me: at our best we were like newlyweds, and at our worst, petulant children. As I arrive at my driveway, Leslie is leaving. I park on the street and get out of my car. Her car's not moving. I see her lay her head down on the steering wheel, and she's crying, waiting for me. I would learn later that someone at the party had called her. I was never sure who, but I have my suspicions.

Though I'm able to coax Leslie back into the house and smooth things over that first time, eventually she will come to accept that a future with Ryan O'Neal is unlikely. Farrah was my future and my past. It was always the present that gave us so much trouble. Our love, though tired and taut, was still alive beneath the rubble of our disillusionment, reaching, pulling, pushing, connecting. Our dance was far from over, but at the time, I was so busy trying to keep ev-eryone happy that I didn't recognize it. And while Farrah

and I continued to feel our way through this floating mé-
lange, our thirteen-year-old would come of age in a world of
uncertainty.

Farrah and I would have other nights like this, when the
need for each other would eclipse our pride, and we'd find
ourselves in irresistible situations. Another night, Leslie was
out of town and Farrah was supposed to join me for dinner
with mutual friends of ours, Freddie and Corina Fields. We
waited and waited for Farrah until we were all so hungry
we ordered dinner without her and hours later went home,
thinking she was a no-show. I was turning out the lights
when Corina called and said that Farrah was on her way
over. "She did end up going to the restaurant and when no
one was there, she came straight here," she continued. "She
wanted to know if you were mad at her."

"What did you tell her?" I asked.

"I told her, yes, but to go over to your house right now.
She'll be there any moment and you be nice to her! You
make her stay over."

I took Corina's advice. Farrah was still captivating. She
was wearing this little black lace bra that was so sexy I insisted she not remove it. I forgave her for being late.

Farrah and I shared joint custody of Redmond. He
was being shuttled back and forth between Farrah's place
and my house on the beach and always preferred the beach,
which irked Farrah. But it was easier for Redmond to stay
with me during the week, near school, and visit his mom

on weekends. At the time, he was attending a public middle school in Malibu. He'd gone to a private elementary school, hated it, and begged us to let him transfer to a "regular" school with "normal kids," and so we gave in. The transfer was a mistake because it coincided with the time the California public school system dropped from best in the country to almost the worst. Our joint custody arrangement was fraught, and I only now appreciate how hard it was on him. Redmond loved Farrah and me equally, and whenever he sensed friction between us, he'd act as the referee. I'd make some offhand critical comment about Farrah, and he'd immediately respond with "Mom didn't mean it that way." And Farrah told me that he did the same thing whenever she offered a rude opinion of me. For a while it worked because he was such an effective goodwill ambassador. But it was far too much to expect that a boy his age could mediate the conflicting interests of two adults, and we were foolhardy to allow him to try. By the time we realized how unfair it was to Redmond, that there were moments when he must have felt as if he were being forced to choose sides, he had already turned away from both of us to a beacon of consolation, his big brother Griffin. By now Griffin was in his early thirties, and was living with me in Malibu. He was teaching Redmond how to play the drums. They formed a band. I had a room downstairs soundproofed for them, thinking, *Isn't it nice? Griffin has taken an interest in his little brother and the two boys are bonding.* But it wasn't nice. Griffin was a drug addict and the worst possible role model to put in front of Redmond. According to the *New York Times,* we now know that most people who become addicted are wired differently from those who do not. Drug addicts seem to have blunted reward systems in the brain, and for them everyday pleasures don't come close to the powerful effects of drugs. However, and for me this is a giant, even people who aren't wired for addiction can become dependent on drugs if they are constantly exposed to them. That summer, between seventh and eighth grade, when Redmond was at his most vulnerable, he was introduced to marijuana. And if anyone could be the poster child for the argument that pot use is dangerous because it leads to harder drugs, it's Redmond.

I knew Griffin was trouble, but I thought that if I let him be there for Redmond, he might feel needed, valued, important. I wanted to save Griffin, but in the end I lost them both. By the time Redmond turned fourteen six months later, he was already getting into trouble with the law, and would be placed in a series of thirteen different juvenile and rehab facilities over the next seven years, all for various drug possession charges.

Farrah and I tried everything: psychiatrists, family counseling, interventions, special schools, and I finally kicked Griffin out of the house. Nothing helped. We watched our son descend into addiction, and we were unable to stop his fall. Like countless other families caught in the same cycle, our situation devolved to the point where we had no choice but to trust in the system and hope that the juvenile court judges and the rehabilitation facilities to which they remanded our child would help him, because we sure couldn't. We believed that these recognized institutions could cure our son. We put our faith in the system. Unfortunately, the very facilities meant to heal kids like Redmond can also accelerate their dependence on drugs.

The nightmare from which we couldn't awake began the following summer, of 1999, before Redmond should have begun his freshman year of high school. He was mixing with the wrong crowd. They were caught smoking pot in the woods by forest rangers. Though he was only issued a citation for a misdemeanor, by now he had a juvenile record—no major crimes, just small teen shenanigans—but the court recognized he was on a downward spiral and mandated that he spend six months in rehab. The judge told Farrah and me that Casa by the Sea was a superior treatment center for teens, and showed us this encouraging video footage of kids in group therapy sitting outside under a beautiful blue sky. Because it seemed too perfect to be possible, I had a bad feeling about the place from the start. But we put our faith in the judge, who, I'll say in her defense, was genuinely concerned for Redmond's welfare and did what she thought was best. I assume she couldn't have known the horrors of this facility. It was on the Mexican border, and when Farrah and I would go down there to visit Redmond, he would tell us disturbing stories about how they were treating the

juveniles confined there, of whom our son was the young-
est. Once, when he refused to apologize for something he
insisted wasn't his fault, he was forced to lie on his stomach for thirty-six hours and was only allowed to get up to
piss. He told us several stories like this and I believed him. I
could see it in his eyes. Farrah thought he was exaggerating
his dire straits so that we'd petition the court for his early
release.

We'd visit him at Casa by the Sea regularly. Sometimes
I'd pick up Farrah from the Wilshire condo, where she was
living; other times we'd drive in separate cars. I saw how the
place was damaging him. His face appeared sunken, as if his
soul were being slowly siphoned away. Farrah wanted him
to remain there. She felt we'd been too lenient with him,
that what he needed was tough love, structure, discipline.
His letters told a different story. There were dozens of them,
each one more heartbreaking than the next. These are a
small sampling:

October 9, 1999

DEAR DAD,
*I got to level three. But now I looked up at the point
sheet and I'm short a point again. It's only one
point dad, honest. It makes me so upset because if
my facilitator's going to drop me back to level two
just because of one single point, then I have to wait*

more time until they let me have a phone call or
be able to walk outside, and other things you only
get on level three. And on level two I have to fast.
They're so strict. Dad please, maybe if you talk to
her tomorrow, my facilitator I mean, Bianca. She's
getting to know me and I hope she didn't take away
my level three. It's only one point. Please you have
to talk to her. Tell her that I need to be on level
three. Dad please. That's it for now.

I love you dad more than you know.

FOREVER,

REDMOND O'NEAL

P.S. I'm in pain. Please write back.

The system at Casa by the Sea was based on points for privileges. He was just a boy and they were denying him food and sunlight. Hardened criminals were treated more humanely. And I know there's much he didn't tell me about what he went through there.

June 4, 2000

DEAR DAD,

I'm back on a really low level again and they won't
let me see you or mom. I'm in solitary now. So I've

been picturing you and mom in my eyes focusing on
you guys and just being home with all of you. It will
take time but I'm only one level away from seeing
you and mom, just one more seminar and about five-
hundred more points and I shall see you once again.
I miss you guys and love you dad more than you'll
ever know.

FOREVER,

REDMOND O'NEAL

P.S. I want to come home. Please write back. I have
goals and I'll work harder. Please I promise.

Even after Redmond was permitted to come home, Farrah insisted he stay there longer, that it was for his own good. Eventually, after being locked up for eighteen months at Casa by the Sea, in December of 2000, what would have been the end of the first semester of his sophomore year of high school, I brought our son home. He was not the same person. Casa by the Sea opened a need inside him and Farrah and I would spend the next decade trying to prevent it from consuming his future. It would push his mother and me apart; it would also be the link that kept us connected. I've recently researched teen drug abuse recidivism, and was impressed by a sad article in *Time*. It's from July 2010. Here's an excerpt:

Living the Dream: Does Teen Drug Rehab Cure
Addiction or Create It?

Increasingly, substance-abuse experts are finding
that teen drug treatment may indeed be doing more
harm than good. The exposure can be especially
dangerous for impressionable youngsters. "I've
known kids who have gone into inpatient treatment
and met other users. After treatment, they meet up
with them and explore new drugs and become more
seriously involved in drug use," says Tom Dishion,
director of research at the Child and Family Center
at the University of Oregon.

It's as if they were writing about Redmond. At eighteen, just a few years after Casa by the Sea, under another
court order and on the heels of having been remanded to
several other facilities in between, Redmond will enter the
Betty Ford Center. Farrah and I were optimistic. This was
the Betty Ford Center, for God's sake. We knew its record
of success. In our case, our child would go in a pot smoker
and occasional pill popper, and come out a heroin addict. He
met a girl there who got him hooked on the stuff. The point
I'm trying to make is that Farrah and I, like so many other
parents in the same impossible situation, wanted desperately
to believe in the merits of the system. It's contradictory that
what starts out as your greatest fear, the sentencing of your

child, ends up being your last hope. When you have failed, you pray the experts have some magic to work. That doesn't mean we as parents are absolved of culpability. It's our job to protect our children and prepare them for the difficulties of adulthood. Redmond always knew that his mom and dad would never deliberately hurt him. But the system would, over and over again. Eventually the *New York Times* would do an exposé on Casa by the Sea, and the Mexican government would shut it down along with three other similar facilities. "See, our son was telling the truth," I wrote Farrah in a note one day that I attached to the article and mailed to her. We never spoke of it again.

For years I blamed Farrah and would quietly seethe every time I thought about how my boy had been trapped in that god-awful place. I was so angry at her, thought she was just being stubborn. At the time, her sculptures were beginning to attract attention in the art world, and part of me thought she had convinced herself it was best for Redmond to stay there because it gave her more time to work in her studio. Now I realize that wasn't why she was so determined not to bring him home. Neither one of us was sure we could handle him, and she knew he'd want to stay at the beach with me. She was afraid for him, of that entire scene, a lifestyle that, in retrospect, I realize may not have been good for any of us. She knew that the permissive teen environment in Malibu was exactly what Redmond didn't need.

He'd run amok with kids his age whose parents were overly indulgent. I think it's why Farrah, as much as she always loved the beach itself, resisted the culture of Malibu.

It took me a long time to understand that a world in which most adults don't work is an odd place for children to grow up in. Most of the time we didn't have the discipline of a regular job, that is, having to get up early in the morning, go to a place of business, answer to other people.

And living aimlessly ain't cheap. Usually, when someone becomes a full-time resident in this oasis by the sea, they don't have to worry about making a living anymore. That was the case for me. Though *Love Story* was a modest payday, I received three million dollars for the sequel, *Oliver's Story*, a handsome sum in the early 1970s. This was before the Julia Robertses and Jim Carreys of the world were paid twenty million a picture. I also made decent money on other films: *The Main Event* and *What's Up Doc*, both of which I starred in with Streisand; *Barry Lyndon*, which Stanley Kubrick directed; and, of course, there was *Paper Moon*. I got thoughtful, conservative advice and invested my earnings wisely. The returns have been handsome.

Though I'm pleased by my financial security, sometimes I wish I'd worked harder for it, taken risks on ventures I believed in, as have many other self-made millionaires. As John Houseman used to say in his famous commercial for Smith Barney, "They make money the old-fashioned way. They earn it." When that commercial first came out thirty-some years ago, I thought, *Why would anyone want to do that if they don't have to?* Now I realize that growing something over time provides the satisfaction of good work well done.

Living in Malibu's casual opulence has been a multiple-decades-long holiday for me. But it came with a price: it eroded my ambition, clouded my introspection, provided such a seductive distraction from the rude competition of Hollywood life, that instead of its being my escape, my haven, it became my confinement.

I remember the afternoon I bought the beach house. This was not long before *Paper Moon* was filmed and Tatum and I had both fallen in love with it. The house, which at the time was a modest cottage on the ocean, was owned by director Blake Edwards, who sold it to me for $130,000. At the time, I thought the price was exorbitant. I renovated the house in stages till it became my idea of home. It's not like one of those huge mansions in East Hampton. It's an open, airy, three-bedroom, two-story contemporary structure with large windows overlooking nothing but blue ocean and sky. In Malibu, most of the beach homes are built close to the shore, so no matter which room you're looking out from, all you see is ocean. It's like being on a houseboat. My favorite part of the house is the master bedroom. Off-white walls, chocolate-colored doors and woodwork, a large bath and dressing rooms, walk-in closets, the Andy Warhol portrait of Farrah over the expansive bed. I love to lie there reading, listening to music. And you can hear the crashing of the

surf. Sometimes, while I'm having my morning coffee, I'll
see a whale surface out of the mist, a school of dolphins, or
maybe a seal bobbing past. There's a large terrace and a
sauna next to the bedroom. Farrah sure loved that sauna.

I have wonderful memories of this beach. Yet sitting
here now, I feel haunted by it. I talk about home and family, but look at what became of my only daughter and me.
While I'm not naive enough to believe all our problems were
caused by where we lived, it wasn't a healthy environment
for an impressionable young girl, any more than it was for
Redmond or Griffin, all three of them limited by their lack
of a decent education. Tatum only had two options: marry a
rich and famous man—and we know how that worked out—
or continue as an actress, but Tatum was never able to make
the transition from the appealing child to the accomplished
adult.

British singer Amy Winehouse died this week. She was
twenty-seven years old and a heroin junkie. I can imagine
what her parents must be going through. And there's still no
guarantee with three of my own four kids. As of the writing
of this book, they're all still here on this earth, thank God.
But addiction, like the devil, is always waiting for that moment when you're at you're weakest, and then he slithers inside and awakens that deadly craving. Patrick is immune to
those temptations. I've never been addicted to anything either, except maybe Farrah. What is this hollow ache that has
so possessed three of my four children? Is it genetic, a con-

sequence of how they were raised, the result of their parents' failure? Sometimes I wish I'd never started this book. Who wants to face these types of questions, when deep down you suspect you already know the answers.

Looking back, I think that's why Farrah became engrossed in her art. Everything in her life had become tentative except her art, which she could physically grasp and hold on to. It gave her comfort and relief because she had charge of it. I now realize it's how she survived our ordeal with Redmond. She poured all her pain into her sculpting the way Judy Garland channeled every hurt through her songs. It was their release, their strength. And Farrah's art was beginning to generate serious attention. A talented young sculptor who was a fan of hers invited Farrah to collaborate with him on an exhibition. Their joint venture examined the relationship between celebrity and fan, and also between projection and reality. Together they created a pair of sculptures: a reclining marble sculpture of her, done mostly by him; and a standing bronze sculpture of him, done mostly by her. They began working on the pieces in the spring of 2000. I've never had a passion for something the way Farrah did for her art. I both envy and admire it. The exhibit premiered at the Los Angeles County Museum of Art to rave reviews in 2002; Rizzoli published a coffee table book about it titled *Recasting Pygmalion;* and a year later the exhibit moved to the Andy Warhol Museum in Pittsburgh, once again garnering critical applause.

I've been rereading *Speak, Memory,* Vladimir Nabokov's remarkable memoir. The author of *Lolita* both inspires me and makes me feel inadequate as I sit here wandering through my own lost time trying to recover images of people and places I adored.

Where were we in our story? Oh yes, the end of year one of the new millennium, when Redmond had just been released from Casa by the Sea. Farrah and I were in a fallow period, having exhausted our emotional and psychological nutrients. It was even taking a toll on my relatively bucolic life with Leslie. Truth be told, I don't remember how I spent the Christmas holidays in 2000. The year before, I spent them with Leslie and her family in Minnesota. I went there with her a couple of Christmases, which were always delightful. I only know that Farrah and I didn't celebrate the 2000 yuletide together because I found a long letter I wrote to her dated December 25, detailing my suggestions on how best we might help Redmond acclimate to being home and suggesting how we might make shared custody more manageable for everyone. I talked about possible schools, getting him excited about music again, a dozen and one ideas. It's not an angry letter. It's full of hope about the future, though once again, Farrah and I were back to communicating via letters and voice mails. I suppose it was to be expected after what we'd just been through with our child. This is how I ended the letter:

I wanted to call but I don't really feel we should try to talk by phone yet. I'll always love you, Farrah, even if I don't always understand you. My fault, I guess. I'm just too slow upstairs, huh? I wish you a merry, merry Christmas and a happy new year, my darling.

Four months later I won't even be sure if I'll see another new year.

CHAPTER NINE

REUNITED

It's April 20, 2001, my sixtieth birthday, and I'm numb. I've just been told I have leukemia when Farrah calls. "You can't die," she says. "We'll fight this together; we'll beat this." We've barely been on speaking terms. I'd actually started to believe her disappointment in me had turned to loathing. But Farrah is weeping and she's never been a crier. That's when I realize, this is lethally serious.

I can envision the headline, "Death Sentence for Ryan O'Neal; Life Imitates Art as Star of *Love Story* Diagnosed with Leukemia." I'm scared and though Farrah and I are estranged, I'm not surprised by her call.

Nothing makes you question your life more than reading about your own mortality, knowing that for once, the newspapers got their facts straight. While my leukemia would eventually go into remission, thanks to a new drug called Gleevec, which was approved for treatment around the time I was diagnosed, in that moment on the phone with her, I could have listed a dozen reasons why she shouldn't be there for me, and only one reason why she should: we were still in love with each other.

I've never been a New Age kind of a guy. Karma,

chakra, abracadabra, it's all the same to me. But lately I've
been starting to rethink my perspective. Maybe the New
Agers are on to something. Look at my old chum George
Hamilton. He's been enlightened since Jimmy' Carter was
president. He's also a genuinely nice guy comfortable with
himself and the world. I envy him that. And then there's
Shirley MacLaine, who seemed to grow younger after she
discovered her past lives, a concept I must admit I do find
romantic. I wonder if Farrah and I were lovers in a past
life. Those who espouse the theory believe that in each lifetime you're given the chance to work out unresolved issues
from a previous life. If that's the case, Farrah and I must
have shared dozens together, and they all began to align that
spring at the dawn of my sixth decade.

It was four years almost to the day that we broke up,
and while admittedly there were good reasons, there were
even more bad excuses. Though I didn't understand it in
1997, it became abundantly clear to me as I began ruminat-
ing about our love affair in the days and weeks following my
diagnosis. Farrah and I each chose the excuses we thought
we needed to flee from each other. We were cowardly, and
now we had no choice but to be brave. My first valiant act
would be accepting the inevitable with Leslie, whom I had
grown to love. Ours wasn't the soul mate version. Farrah always occupied that part of me. But Leslie was kind and her
generosity boundless. As much as I wanted to be back with
Farrah, it was still hard letting go of this appealing young

woman who embodied qualities I wished that my daughter exhibited. Leslie was with me when the oncologist broke the news. She was in the room when the doctors inserted this enormous needle into my spine to extract a bone marrow sample. They needed cells to confirm the type of leukemia. The pain was excruciating. I almost came off the table twice and had to be held down. They pumped me with pain meds until finally they got what they needed. I couldn't walk afterward. I went in there a strapping guy and I came out in a wheelchair. Leslie witnessed all of this, and I think it got to her, not that she wouldn't have been there for me through the long haul. She would have because she was caring and unselfish, but by then she'd met actor James Spader on location for a film. They'd eventually marry and have children. Leslie thought it best to exit gracefully, and I've always admired her for that.

My second act of bravery was to occur when I got home from the doctor's office. Tatum showed up because she'd heard the death knell. I wasn't expecting much by way of sympathy, but I sure wasn't ready for what I got. She verbally stripped me bare, recounting the highlights of my failed life and then, before slamming the door on her way out, she said, "Well, at least my mother died with dignity." I worry that if that episode in our lives comes up on the reality show, I won't be able to manage it. But then nothing should surprise me. I didn't get a call on my fiftieth birthday either.

While one of my children was sticking in the knife that

spring, another was twisting it. Griffin was back in jail. He had been up to his old tricks: more high-speed car chases, more guns, more violence. Only this time when the cops had him cornered, he attempted suicide by police. I didn't believe it at first until several months later when I saw it in a letter he wrote me from prison. He was in solitary twenty-three hours a day for thirty-six weeks. His words still haunt me: "I begged the officer to shoot but he didn't." Cancer patients often say their illness makes them feel helpless. I can assure you that nothing makes you feel as helpless as your adult children sabotaging their own futures. When they're little, you can exert discipline, protect them. Then they hit an age when despite how desperately you want to save them from themselves, you can't. I asked Farrah once, "If we had never separated, do you think Redmond would still have gotten into trouble?"

She didn't answer. Maybe because she knew the answer was yes.

By the time Leslie and I broke up in 2001, Farrah and I had been driving back and forth to visit Redmond at various facilities for several years, a ritual we would sadly have to keep repeating and that I continue to this day. Some of the places where Redmond was staying were located in isolated areas where there were more tumbleweeds than streetlights. I'd do whatever I could to keep our spirits up. I'd take her to a local movie theater, or we'd find rustic restaurants and cafés. We'd try to see the humor in our bizarre circumstance. And believe me, we encountered our fair share of bizarre. Some of these camps asked parents to participate in group therapy sessions that often included weird rituals led by wacko facilitators. These activities were meant to strip us of our defense mechanisms. It never worked on me. I remember one so-called group leader who insisted that a couple pick another member of the group, lift the person off the floor, and swing him or her around so he or she could experience "flying." I'm not embellishing. Remember that famous scene from *Titanic* in which Leonardo DiCaprio holds Kate Winslet as she leans forward on the bow of the ship and tells her she's flying? That's what we had to do except there was no wind, no boat, no ocean, and no James Cameron, just green linoleum and gray walls. One time Farrah and I were attending another group encounter and the facilitator, who was a double for Nurse Ratched from *One Flew Over the Cuckoo's Nest*, told Farrah she had to take off her sunglasses. Farrah was sporting a nasty sty in her right eye that day. The woman was insistent, even going so far as to try to remove the glasses from Farrah's face. I thought Farrah was going to take the woman down. Instead she smiled demurely and said: "Touch my Maui Jims and your hand will come back without fingers." The facilitator retreated. I glimpsed Farrah winking at me behind those glasses. It was the tiny triumphs that kept us going. The big ones were much fewer and farther between.

I'd like to believe that it wasn't the leukemia that brought

Farrah and me back together. Farrah had begun to mellow. Gone was the frustrated, angry woman. Replacing her was this patient person who seemed comfortable inside her own skin. Maybe we both had grown up. Still, reconciliation didn't happen quickly. It would take time for us to trust each other again, something Mia and Frank could never do. This might be a good time to lighten things up a bit and tell you that story.

The year, 1965. The place, 20th Century Fox Studios. Mia and I are on lunch break from *Peyton Place*. We're walking to the commissary. We pass the set of *Von Ryan's Express*, a movie about escaped prisoners of war in which Sinatra is starring. Fencing designed to imitate barbed wire surrounds the set. The effect is so realistic, it's as if we're standing in front of a POW camp. The cast is milling about. Mia asks me to point out which of the actors is Sinatra. "I can't spot him," I say. Suddenly a gate at the other end of the set opens and a golf cart piled with six guys in army fatigues pulls out. "Look at the driver," I whisper to her. "That's Sinatra." I watch her face. I can almost hear the lyrics to "I've Got a Crush on You" playing in her head. A couple days later back on the set of *Peyton Place*, Mia pulls me aside. "I had the privilege of meeting Mr. Frank Sinatra yesterday," she says. I asked her how she found the time. Our production schedule had been grueling the day before. "They were shooting interiors on the next stage and I just walked over and introduced myself," she answers. I was even more perplexed.

"You met Frank Sinatra in a hospital gown?" *Peyton Place* was shooting hospital scenes that week. "No, I put on a robe and slippers first."

She was nineteen years old. He was forty-eight. They wed two years later. I was married to Patrick's mother, Leigh Taylor-Young, at the time. We enjoyed many evenings with Mr. and Mrs. Sinatra. They were wonderful to us. Frank liked having his friends around and what a cast of pals they were: fellow rat packers Dean Martin; Joey Bishop; Sammy Davis, Jr.; childhood friend Jilly Rizzo, known as much for his ties to Mulberry Street as for his eponymous eaterie; comedian Shecky Greene; actor Brad Dexter. And what you have to understand is that these men were old school, Frank especially. Not always the easiest environment for a serious-minded young bride with a Hollywood pedigree. Mia's father, John Farrow, was a respected Australian-born film director and her mother was famed Irish-born actress Maureen O'Sullivan.

Don't get me wrong. I loved Frank. He could be a gentleman. But he had an uncontrollable jealous streak. One night Leigh and I were driving down Sunset Boulevard on my motorcycle. We'd just had a lovely dinner with Jacqueline Bisset and her partner of many years, Michael Sarrazin. He was a wonderful actor. Anyway, Leigh and I are on the bike when suddenly someone whooshes past us in a Dual Ghia. This is an expensive Italian sports car and there weren't too many of them on the road. I knew that Frank had one.

There's a red light ahead of us and I see the Ghia come to a screeching halt behind another car. I drive up alongside the Ghia, and Leigh and I glance to our right. Sure enough, it's Frank at the wheel, and sitting next to him in the passenger side is Mia. They don't see us. Mia's hands are clasped tightly on her lap and she's sitting there rigid. She looks terrified. It's a long red. Frank can't wait. He wheels out from behind the other driver, nearly sideswiping him, and runs the light.

The next afternoon, Leigh and I are expected at their home for Sunday brunch. When we arrive, there are large pieces of furniture all over the front yard: an armoire, a dresser, a hand-carved desk, custom cabinets, even a piano. It looks as if an absentminded auctioneer started to set up for an estate sale, said "Aw, the hell with it," and left. I ask myself, *At only five foot nine and a hundred and forty-five pounds, could Frank possibly have dragged all this furniture out of the house by himself?* The adrenaline must have been really flowing. But I heard he didn't like the way the owner of the antique shop looked at his wife when she purchased that furniture. And Frank was a very possessive man.

Though Mia and Frank's marriage survived only a few years, their friendship would endure a lifetime. He loved her and she loved him, but he couldn't own her. She was her own girl then, and an exquisite woman now. I still hear from Mia from time to time. After Farrah died, she sent me a beautiful letter that only someone of her depth and grace could have written. Leigh had replaced Mia on *Peyton Place* in 1966. We were married the next year in Hawaii. Leigh was pregnant with Patrick and chose to leave our prime-time soap, which wasn't making good use of her considerable talent. Patrick is now a well-regarded sportscaster in LA. We speak frequently. I salute him and bow to Leigh, who has been as good a mother as she was an actress.

Thinking about Frank Sinatra is a painful reminder of my own jealous streak. Back in 2001 when I found out I had leukemia and Farrah rushed to my side, there was a part of me that was still smarting from her affair with James Orr. I wish I could say I was man enough to let it go, but I wasn't. It would take being told I might die of cancer for me to finally move past it. And I thought *Farrah* was stubborn. All these years I let her infidelity eat away at me, and though we never did speak of it after my diagnosis, I forgave her in my heart because reconciling meant more to me than holding on to something that was over and done with. While I was writing Chapter Six of this book, I asked Farrah's archivist to see if he could find any of the call sheets from *Man of the House* because I wanted to try to confirm as best as I could the exact production dates. He couldn't find her calendar. What he did find was more important: Redmond's summer reading list from that year: *Treasure Island, The Adventures of Tom Sawyer, The Secret Garden.* It's full of notes in Farrah's handwriting on his progress with each book. Redmond spent his summer break in 1994 on location with Farrah. He was with her the entire time. I don't know why I didn't remember that. And when she begged me to believe her that nothing had happened with Orr, why didn't I realize then that Farrah would never have had an affair with her son present.

All that agony for nothing. She was telling the truth.

What a revelation: our second chance wasn't just because I got sick. It wasn't even only for Redmond. Though a heavy new burden is handed to me--the knowledge that the woman I loved died thinking I believed she had been unfaithful—another is lifted.

As 2001 churns forward and the specter of my mortality recedes into the wormhole of memory, Farrah and I slowly find our way back to that comfortable place we thought could never be recaptured. She moves part-time into the beach house and occupies the bedroom across from mine. As fate often dictates, I had just added a third bedroom upstairs, never imagining it would become Farrah's room.

When you love somebody, you cherish their signature quirks. One for me was Farrah's sleeping habits. Once when she was about ten, her family—her mother, father, and sister—was going to a drive-in. She got in the car first and fell asleep. They drove to the drive-in and saw two movies while she slept. When they got home and parked in the driveway, she wakes up and says, "Well, I guess we're not going." And those qualities stayed with her. When she'd take a nap, there'd be this tiny indentation on one side and the rest of the bed would be untouched. You wouldn't even have to remake it afterward, just smooth over one side of the covers. She could sleep anywhere, airplanes or cars; the moment her head touched the pillow, she'd be out just like a little girl.

During our estrangement, I had forgotten some of these appealing aspects of Farrah's personality. Perhaps it was my way of coping with our having lost each other: I wouldn't let myself remember anything endearing because it hurt too much. Once Farrah reenters my life in 2001, all the delightful qualities of hers that I'd been blocking come flooding back. Farrah had a whimsical side that could be infuriating one moment, and enchanting the next. For instance, she loved to wiggle her way into my physical exams. Once, when we were at my oncologist's office and he was examining me, Farrah, ever so sweetly and with this coquettish smile, lifts up her arm and says in her best Texas drawl, "Doctor, this wouldn't happen to be a little old lymph node would it?" You could almost hear the batting of her eyelashes. And of course, he's soon attending to the spot on her arm while I'm sitting there with my shirt off, waiting for him to check *my* lymph nodes. The same thing happened years before when Farrah was in her ninth month of pregnancy with Redmond. I had a chicken-eye corn between my toes. Farrah is there and the doctor and I are discussing whether it's best to treat it topically with ointments or get it surgically removed. Suddenly Farrah is kicking off her shoes, and then hoisting her leg onto the examining table (no easy feat at nine months along), saying, "Doctor, would you take a look at these nasty old warts on my foot?" Within minutes he's abandoned me and is removing them for her. Both she and I believed it was the foot doctor who brought on her labor because only hours later her water broke. Back then, these sorts of things made me chuckle.

And in 2001 I was relieved to know that Farrah still had that connection to me, that it had never died; it was just asleep for a while the same way she had been that night at the drive-in movie. Now we were both awake and our love had deepened. Farrah had forgiven me for Leslie. She had finally come to understand why I had gone.

While I'm recuperating, Farrah's still busy preparing for her art exhibit. She had recently sold the house on Antelo and moved into a spacious condo in an exclusive building on Wilshire Boulevard, which also doubled as her studio. In addition to her art projects, she's starring in episodes of *Spin City*. She played a judge and she was delightful in the part. Her comic timing was spot on. Interestingly enough, during this time Farrah had found some old episodes of *Good Sports* on video and we watched them together. "You know, that show wasn't half bad," she said. "We were better together than we thought." I smiled: we always were.

I've been so immersed in reminiscing that it just

occurred to me: 2001 was the year of 9/11. Farrah was filming in LA and tending Redmond. I was in Istanbul with
Freddie and Corina Fields. We had been in Greece when
Freddie got an invitation to visit Turkey from a woman he
thought might finance a movie. I was doubtful but having
read Eric Ambler's *A Coffin for Dimitrios,* I wanted to see
Istanbul. The first night, I was having a drink at the bar.
This lovely young American woman on holiday starts chatting with me. It was a sweet conversation between two tour-
ists, but by the second glass of wine, she began hinting at
something more, and having just gotten back on the mend
with Farrah, the last thing I wanted was a Mediterranean
fling. So I politely excused myself. The next morning I'm
in the hotel restaurant reading the breakfast menu and she's
sitting with her luggage at the table next to me. She asks me
to join her, which I do. Not the smartest thing, I know, but
she was a nice woman, I didn't want to hurt her feelings,
and I felt bad about the night before. We order breakfast and
she tells me she's flying to New York in a few hours for an
important job interview. "But I could push it back and fly
tomorrow instead," she suggests. "Then we could spend the
day together." I gently tell her no, that she needs to make it
to her interview as scheduled, and I need to stop talking to
pretty girls. She kept trying to change my mind. "Come on,
I've never done anything spontaneous like this before and
I may never get the chance to again," she said. We finished

breakfast and I helped her with her bags and watched her get into a cab for the airport.

That was September 10, 2001. Her interview was at 8:30 a.m. at the World Trade Center the following morning.

It was early evening the next day in Istanbul. I'm dressing when Freddie calls saying to turn on CNN, which I do, just as the second plane hits the second tower. My first thought was for my family, all of whom I immediately tried to call, and would be dialing for hours before I would finally be able to get an open line. All the while, in my mind's eye, I kept flashing back to an image of that girl. Freddie and I were supposed to attend a dinner party that night. I bowed out. He later told me that when he arrived, the hostess said the terrorists were Japanese, as was being reported on Turkish radio and television, not Muslims.

While the death toll in New York punctuated that year for every American, Farrah had to face one much closer to home. On October 16, her beloved older sister, Diane, died of cancer at sixty-two years old. Not a good number for the Fawcetts.

Our lives would continue to be driven by ups and downs both personally and professionally. In 2002, following her successful stint on *Spin City*, Farrah's television career would see another resurgence with four appearances on the hit legal drama *The Guardian*. Her portrayal was of a troubled single grandmother, for which she received another

Emmy nomination, her fifth. That's when I realized how far she'd come since the weeks and months leading to her fiftieth birthday. Before, it would have eaten at her that she was being cast as a grandma; whereas now, not only did she take it in stride, she had come to appreciate her age and had even begun to enjoy the early rewards of maturity. For me, Farrah accepting that role in *The Guardian* and inhabiting it with such aplomb was her homecoming to herself.

My career was sputtering along like that old Model T Mose drove in *Paper Moon*. Around the same time Farrah was taping *The Guardian*, I was in production for the film *People I Know*, with Al Pacino. It's about a slick New York press agent whose actor client gets himself into a publicity mess that he has to clean up. I play the actor. Yes, I do see the irony. And no, not even Pacino was enough to save this movie when it was released in May of the following year. I'm like a homing pigeon for embarrassing footnotes to the careers of the otherwise ridiculously successful. I wonder if it's a gypsy curse.

And my good luck would just keep on coming. The following fall, in 2004, Tatum releases her autobiography titled *A Paper Life*. A mess on paper is more like it. I didn't read it when it came out in hardcover, and not only because my friends warned it would make me unhappy. I figured I'd heard it all before. So I can't recommend that you buy it. Though I may seem to be making light of my daughter's memoir, the truth is, it did hurt.

Despite whatever setbacks we were facing in any given moment, whether they were troubles with Redmond or my other children or our jobs, Farrah and I were growing stronger together, and our relationship, though still not completely healed from the wounds of years past, was becoming more elastic and able to bend without breaking. By the end of 2004, the tabloids had been hinting for more than a year of a Fawcett-O'Neal wedding. Sometimes we'd curl up on the couch at the beach house and read each other the articles.

During this period, the cable network TV Land offered Farrah a million dollars to do a day-to-day reality series called *Chasing Farrah*. This was long before reality mania, and I had reservations about unrehearsed exposure, but she was intrigued by the idea and wanted to give it a try, so I supported her decision. I even agreed to be in an episode. We taped it at the beach house. When I watch it now, I see just how remarkable Farrah and I were together. The footage of us at the beach—her sitting on my lap while I smiled and kissed her—would look to anyone who didn't know our story as if we had never been apart.

The series ran for only seven episodes before being canceled, but it was worth it for Farrah. It established her as a dignified pioneer of an emerging television genre, and it also gave her the chance to honor her love for her mother. In March of 2005, Farrah and the crew went to Texas to tape an episode with her family. Pauline, whose health was failing, was able to take part. She died weeks later, with Farrah knowing how proud she was of her daughter.

I lost my mother in 2005 too. She was ninety-five. I'll never forget the year before when my brother called to tell me it was time. Mom was leaving us. She was in the hospital then and had been there for a while, never having recovered from hip replacement. After the surgery, she began to fade away and my brother and I were living in that awful limbo of "any-day-now-speak" that the doctors give you. When I arrived at her bedside, her breathing was shallow and her pulse was faint. Kevin and I kissed her hand, told her we loved her, told her what she meant to us and how important she was in our lives. Mom was in an older wing of the hospital and there was a fire exit outside her room. Kevin and I sat on the steps and we reminisced about our life with her. We laughed and told stories. Then we went back inside. I held her in my arms, and I said good-bye to my beloved mother. The next morning, I got another call from Kevin.

"She's back," he says.

"Who's back?" I ask.

"Mom!" Kevin replies.

"Mom? You mean she's still alive?"

"Yes, she's right here," he says. "Do you want to talk to her?"

She'd rallied. My mom had apparently decided she would live another year, so she did. It was in character. For decades she had personally answered all of Tatum's and my fan mail, always making sure that every person who took the time to write was given the courtesy of a thoughtful response. I still miss her.

As the year comes to a close, I'm given an uplifting surprise. The producers of *Desperate Housewives* invite me to make a guest appearance as character Lynette Scavo's father-in-law. I happily accept. I always liked the sardonic wit of that show and who wouldn't want to spend a day with that gorgeous cast?

The holidays are thankfully uneventful.

2006 begins innocuously. It will not end that way.

CHAPTER TEN

THE LAST MYSTERY

It's autumn of 2006. Farrah and I are lying in bed at the beach house. I see her considering her legs. "Is one of my thighs bigger than the other?" she says. "Of course not," I reply. She points to her right leg. "This one is larger," she insists. Humoring her, I take the tape measure out of the dresser drawer and measure both her thighs. She's right. One is an inch larger than the other. "Something's wrong with me," she says. "No, no, you're fine," I tell her. But she wasn't. Her body was retaining fluid. Since the death of her mom the year before, Farrah had been feeling exhausted and was sleeping far more than usual, but we both assumed it was the grieving process and that it would eventually pass. It never occurred to either of us that she was sick. After all, I was the one with cancer. It seemed inconceivable we could both be struck by lightning.

But on September 22, Farrah is diagnosed with a rare and aggressive form of cancer and told to get her affairs in order. For the next two and a half years we will fight to save her life. And as the battle unfolds, we will be given the unexpected gift that anyone who's ever known love often receives too late. We will learn why you must give everything you've got now, this minute, because when that moment passes, so too may your chance to keep the promises you've spent a lifetime making. What you're about to read are my reflections on those days as we waged war on her cancer and opened that profound gift.

As word began to spread that Farrah was sick, the press became as invasive as her disease. It would become a race to try to update family and friends on her condition before they read it in the newspapers. We wouldn't always win that race. Making matters worse, the papers portrayed Farrah as already having relinquished hope. The front page of the *National Enquirer* read: "Farrah Begs, Let Me Die." Eventually we will orchestrate a trap and catch the hospital employee who was feeding Farrah's medical records to the media. Our aggressive stance will spark new legislation protecting the privacy rights of patients, and Governor Schwarzenegger will sign it into law.

In the wake of Farrah's diagnosis in 2006, as fall turned to winter, we weren't thinking about beating the tabloids; we were too busy trying to figure out how to destroy the malignant tumor growing inside her. We were diligent, consulting doctor after doctor, trying to cut our way through the dense foliage of medicalspeak to understand each opinion, weigh every option, and make the right decisions. Every oncologist was offering us a chalice. Which one was Farrah's Holy Grail? While doctors didn't always agree on the most effective course of action to eradicate her tumor, they shared a similar opinion on her prognosis. In *Dark Victory,* a Bette Davis film about a woman who discovers she's terminally ill at the prime of her life, there's a scene in which Davis suspects her doctor is withholding the truth, so she sneaks a look at her test results and sees "prognosis negative." She reads the words out loud and you can watch her trying to digest their meaning. The rest of the film is about her dying with dignity. Farrah was given the same prognosis, but for her it was all about *living.* Farrah's determination to conquer the odds will be contagious, and it will not only inspire those closest to her; it will motivate a generation of cancer patients to never lose hope, to keep reaching for life. For thirty-three months Farrah will endure a debilitating series of treatments and procedures. She will travel back and forth to Germany for treatments not yet available in the States. She'll work with doctors at UCLA, Saint John's Health Center, and City of Hope. And through it all, she never stops fighting. Her desperate struggle to survive wasn't only because she wanted to live; it was also because she *needed* to live to protect her son and to fulfill the promise of our love for each other. And in February of 2007, Farrah and I would be celebrating a report that the initial treatments had worked and that she was cancer free. I told her that we were going back to the Pierre this time for sure, two weeks at least. She remembered and smiled. "I can't wait to get on that plane with you."

It was February 4, two days after Farrah's fifty-ninth birthday. We were dining with her oncologist, drinking champagne and toasting the birthday girl's reprieve. It was a joyous evening, full of laughter and engaging conversation. And for the first time in more than four months there was no talk of cancer. We discussed Farrah's art and a script that she was interested in. We chatted about my new recurring role on the popular series *Bones*, marveling over the fact that the producers had cast me as a priest. But mostly we spoke of the future. It had been returned to us just hours earlier when we received the call that the tumor was gone. We were fully alive that night. Our love and our future were vibrant again, revitalized by gratitude.

Though we believed Farrah was safe, we would never make it back to the Pierre. We needed to save our son, who had become addicted to heroin. Though we'd been honest with him about Farrah's cancer, we were protecting him from the details as much as we could because he was in such a delicate state in what we thought was recovery. We didn't want to leave him alone that night because he wasn't strong enough to be trusted, so I asked Griffin if he would stay with his brother while Farrah and I went out for the evening. Griffin had supposedly been clean and sober for a year. I figured that if anyone could prevent Redmond from sneaking out in search of drugs, it would be Grif, who knows every subterfuge there is. His girlfriend was pregnant and he was jubilant about having a baby. Griffin had been domesticated. He had been doing well, and I was proud of him. It had been so long since I'd felt that way toward my oldest son that I let it blind me. When I left the beach house to meet Farrah, Redmond was sound asleep, and Griffin was watching TV with his girlfriend and their dog. A few hours later, my tranquil sanctuary would turn into a parody of a Stephen King novel. I'll spare you all the ridiculous details and just give you the high points.

After dinner, I drop Farrah off at her condo on Wilshire and drive back to the beach. When I arrive, the scene before me is chaos spiked with insanity. The house is a disaster area. Griffin has tied and gagged Redmond to keep him from leaving in search of drugs. I tell Griffin to free his brother while I call Farrah. Tempers are igniting. I order Griffin to leave. He won't go. I reach for a fireplace poker. At this point I'm afraid of Griffin. He yanks the poker out of my hand and swings it at my face. I duck. He swings again, hitting me in the knee. A flash of pain shoots up my leg. Incredulous, I hobble upstairs to my bedroom where I keep a licensed gun for emergencies—and this sure was an emergency. I fire a warning shot into the wall. It works the same way it does in those old cowboy movies: everyone stops screaming and is still for a moment. Then Griffin runs outside and calls 911, crying "Shots fired, shots fired." Soon there are squad cars everywhere, the Pacific Coast Highway has been closed, and a helicopter hovers overhead. "Come out with your hands up," someone shouts. At first I ask myself, *Is this the police or the second assistant director talking*? I'm soon disabused of the fantasy that this is only a movie. I'm frisked, handcuffed, read my Miranda rights, put in the backseat of a police car, and while sirens scream, am taken to central booking, where an infamous mug shot is snapped that will pollute the pages of every grocery store publication except *Better Homes and Gardens.* The district attorney, who knew Griffin's criminal history, releases me because of insufficient evidence and all charges are dropped. The arrest made headlines. My being found innocent of any wrongdoing didn't even make the local *Penny Saver.* The next morning I do what I should have done a long time ago: I cut Griffin off for good. Really, at forty-two years old he should make his own car payments, pay his own rent, take out his own insurance. And he can buy his own paper towels.

Fast-forward three months to May 2007. Redmond is back in treatment. Farrah and I are just starting to breathe again when her doctors call. The cancer is back and it's me-tastasized. So much has been written of Farrah's fight to live. Alana Stewart wrote a moving book about their experiences in those dark but meaningful months. And it's likely you're familiar with the documentary *Farrah's Story,* which aired on NBC and chronicled the final two and a half years of Farrah's life. I don't want to repeat what's already been covered. I want you to know what's in here (I'm pointing at my heart). Though Farrah shared her struggle with the world, there are aspects of what she went through that have not been written about or captured on camera, moments that belonged to us alone.

It was Alana who found the clinic in Germany. The

Best girlfriends Alana and Farrah on my fifty-third birthday. Alana was Farrah's guardian angel till the very end.

doctors there had had success with Farrah's form of cancer in the past and were optimistic about treating her. There was one catch: the procedures would be radical and she could end up spending the time she had left suffering instead of living. She and Alana were encouraged. I was terrified. I don't remember how soon we got on a plane to Germany, but it seems to me it was almost overnight. All during the flight, I was on edge. I needed to be there for Farrah, but I was also worried about Redmond. Though we had family friends keeping an eye on him in LA and he would be joining us in Germany soon, I continued to fear the worst. Farrah and Alana would travel back and forth to Germany six times between 2007 and 2009. I would go only twice and not because I had abandoned Farrah, as the press would cry in outrage, but because I'd promised Farrah I wouldn't leave our son, who was also fighting for his life.

It became apparent how bad off Redmond was when he arrived in Germany. Alana's ex-husband and our dear friend, George Hamilton, accompanied him from LA. The moment I saw Red's face, I knew. He had the eyes of an old man, and there was an emptiness that seemed to go on forever inside him. He stayed for three weeks. I barely slept. While doctors were injecting powerful toxins into Farrah's bloodstream with needles the size of tuning forks, and she lay in bed crying, vomiting, wanting to go home, I was running between her bedside and our hotel room, making sure Redmond wasn't using. Then I found a blackened spoon in the sink. Part of me wanted to throttle him, but I knew his was a disease every bit as insidious as his mother's cancer. When I read my journal entries from that period, I can feel my chest tighten.

JOURNAL ENTRY, JUNE 12, 2007
I'm so scared. Red shows up and looks gaunt and lost. I take him to lunch but he hardly eats. I'm worried he's sliding into the abyss. I beg him to think about his mother's health. It's her time right now, not his or mine, hers. But I'm not sure he can control his destiny anymore. I may lose them both.

The two people I loved most on earth were both sick and every hour of every day I was reminded of how powerless I was to save either of them. I even started praying again, pleading with God to take me instead. I existed in this tiny space in my head where disbelief, despair, hope, and rage all intersected, and sometimes I became squeezed in so tight I couldn't breathe. That's when Farrah's courage, her grace in the face of life's last mystery, and her strong faith became my oxygen. She thought I was there to give her strength, but it was she who was the provider. And though our time at the clinic was frightening, there were beautiful moments too, moments that changed the way I looked at life. I had never been around such illness before, illness that permeates a place where people come as their last hope. Most days I was so immersed in what was happening to Farrah and the ghost of what used to be my son, I didn't possess the selflessness to notice we weren't the only family lost in Plato's cave.

JOURNAL ENTRY, JUNE 23, 2007
The wife of a terminally ill patient asked if I would meet a young German woman who is stricken with an unpronounceable illness. I visited with the young woman for a long time. She asked me to autograph a photo. She's in a wheelchair and I pushed her back to her room, which looks out onto the Alps and the lush farmland that surrounds this part of Bavaria. She's a dear dying girl and I held her in my arms when she became emotional. A fan of *Love Story,* she has seen it many, many times. I hope I made her feel a

little better. I stop in to see my other girl, but she's
already sleeping. It's been a hard journey . . .

That's why Farrah filmed that journey, to flood the cave
with light. She wanted to bring cancer and the reality of
what cancer patients have to go through to the public eye.
She didn't want the side effects of chemotherapy to be hidden like some shameful secret. She wanted to show everyone
the dignity behind every patient's struggle to beat cancer.
She asked Alana to film her to demystify the horrors, to
confront and diminish the stigma, and to generate awareness
and support for patients who can't afford the most effective
treatment and so will never know the privilege of hope. She
wasn't unlike Pope John Paul II, who courageously continued to say Mass every Sunday despite being in the advanced
stages of Parkinson's disease. When Vatican advisers began
pressuring him not to appear in public because they thought
it undignified for a pontiff to drool and tremble as he led the
world in prayer, he refused, admonishing his advisers: "This
too is part of life." Farrah didn't think she would die when
she began the documentary. She thought it would be a testi-
monial to survival. Instead it would become so much more.
But that spring of 2007, when Alana began videotaping, we
were all still hopeful a miracle was coming.

Farrah returns home in late June visibly weakened. She
will be in and out of the hospital all summer and eventually

have to return to Germany in September and then again in November for more treatments. Meanwhile, I'm doing everything I can to help Redmond navigate his perils with the law. His drug addiction has withered his character to the point where he is barely recognizable to himself or his family, and I'm afraid that soon mandated rehab won't satisfy the courts. Redmond is stoic but underneath I know my son is scared, and he hates that he keeps disappointing his mother and me with his relapses, but we've tried every rehab program out there—twelve steps, fifty steps, forty turns—it doesn't matter; they don't work for him. And like every addict, he wants to reclaim his life, but when he reaches out his arms to grab hold of it, he trips and tumbles backward.

It was a cruel autumn. I trudged through the days, head down, trying not to lose my patience with family and friends who meant well but whose attempts to help often put me more on edge. It wasn't that I didn't need or want the support; I was desperate for it. But like the character Lon Chaney, Jr., played in *The Werewolf*, sometimes it was safer for everyone if I kept to myself. The Christmas holidays were overcast with the precariousness of our future. Farrah was back home, and though thin and pale, she still had that smile. It was like sunshine for me. On Christmas morning we exchanged presents. This was the card attached to her gift for Redmond, which I've held for safekeeping. Sometimes when I feel myself starting to lose perspective, I take it out and let her words to her son center me.

December 25, 2007

MY DARLING REDMOND,

It is important that you know, not only on this
Christmas day, but in all the days since you were born
and in all the years that follow, you, sweet boy, are
the love of my life. My most special gift from God.
I look at life differently now since I became ill. I look
at every day with appreciation and gratefulness. It
changed my outlook knowing that life could be taken
away so easily. There is a quote that has more meaning
to me now and I hope you will be able to use it at
twenty-two years old instead of sixty years old. "You
don't get to choose how or when you're going to die.
You can only decide how you're going to live."

So my sweet boy, I wanted to make a sculpture
especially for you. I thought I would always have time
but I realized I must do what is truly special for the
ones I love now. I don't want any regrets because I
waited too long. Life is a miraculous gift and as your
mother I want to guide you to appreciate yours.

You are blessed in so many ways and must
never forget how special you are.

I'll love you forever.
I'll like you for always.
As long as I'm living my baby you'll be.

WITH ALL MY HEART,

MOTHER

Farrah also gave me a sculpture that year. It's a female torso with rich, sensual curves. I keep it on the mantle in my bedroom and sometimes when I hold it, I can feel her presence.

The last three lines in her letter to Redmond come from a famous bedtime story written by Robert Munsch and illustrated by Sheila McGraw titled *Love You Forever*. It's about a mother loving her child through all the stages of growing up, from the cooing infant phase and the terrible twos all the way to adulthood. In each scene, no matter how much the boy tries the mother's patience, she steals into his room at night after he's asleep and holds him in her arms, whispering "I'll love you forever. I'll like you for always. As long as I'm living my baby you'll be." Farrah used to read that bedtime story to Redmond when he was a baby. She usually concluded anything she wrote to him with those words, whether it was a note tacked to the refrigerator reminding him to study for his spelling test, or one of the many long letters he received from her during his stints in rehab or jail. At the end of the bedtime story, the mother is old and dying, and the son, now a grown man, goes into her room while she's sleeping and takes her in his arms reciting those beloved lines. Redmond would never get that chance, which is why I've kept every note, every letter to him from Farrah in the hope that someday when he's ready to read them, he will feel her protective presence the same way I do when I hold that sculpture.

By January of 2008, Farrah would once again have to

travel to Germany for more procedures but she would return home within weeks. Her body was being ravaged by
medical treatments intended to save her, while her cancer
was growing stronger and more invasive. Her doctors an-
guished over what to do to give her a chance of survival. She
never gave up. Her oncologists were impressed by her re-
lentless determination to live. So as the doctors labored on,
Alana, under strict instructions from Farrah, kept the video
camera rolling. Farrah would not wave that white flag yet.

Back in LA, I was dealing with Redmond and doing
everything I could to keep the truth from Farrah because
I was afraid in her frail state, knowing her son was careen-
ing toward possible imprisonment, it would be too much for
her to withstand. In the months following January of 2008,
it was as if all of us were living out a play by Eugene Ionesco
from the Theater of the Absurd, where nothing makes sense
and the characters keep turning in circles. That January,
Redmond got in trouble again; only this time, by the spring
of 2009, he would find himself behind bars. Less than six
months earlier, in June of 2008, Tatum would be busted in
New York City for buying crack cocaine, and our family
would once again be fodder for the headline hunters. And
before the ink used on that story was dry, the newspapers
were handed their next ugly installment. In September of
2008 the police raided my house in Malibu early one morning as part of a court-mandated check on Redmond, who was
on parole. Farrah was back home by then and was sleeping

upstairs when they descended upon us. They ransacked the place, determined to unearth something, and they did. Before I went to bed the night before I had found a packet of crystal meth in Redmond's room. He told me it wasn't his, that he was holding it for a friend at Pepperdine, the college up the road. I know, a likely story, so I took it from him and hid it in my shoe under my bed, thinking I'd dispose of it the next morning. The police came before I had a chance. It turned out that the crystal meth was a diversionary tactic. I'd assumed that's all Red had. The police made no such assumption. They found his stash. We would both be booked and prosecuted. Two months later, to protect Redmond, I would plead guilty to possession of crystal meth and be sentenced to attend outpatient drug management sessions. I had asserted ownership of the meth when the police first found it, thinking the court would go lighter on Redmond. In retrospect, it didn't help him and only further sullied my reputation, if such a downgrade was possible. If all of this wasn't so tragic, it would be funny. First the press tells the world I tried to shoot one of my kids. Then I'm the reason my daughter is on crack. And now I'm a tweeking meth addict who hides drugs in his loafers. I won't be offended if you're trying not to laugh. And next, I'll be accused of "elder abuse." That's right. You did hear me correctly.

I call him Nevius the Devious. His real name is Craig Nevius, and he worked with Farrah on her reality series *Chasing Farrah*. Now he was supposed to be helping Alana and Farrah transform their raw footage of Farrah's illness into a two-hour prime-time documentary special for NBC. But soon we realized he was in over his head. It was now spring of 2009, Farrah was back home from what would be her final trip to Germany, and with every tick of the clock she was growing weaker. When Farrah, Alana, and I watched Nevius's rough cut of the documentary, we were dumbstruck. It was amateur night. It was incoherent, badly paced, and missed the point of why Farrah wanted her illness made public. Farrah pleaded with me to step in and take over the project with Alana, and within days, at Farrah's behest, the proper papers had been drawn and signed. Nevius went apoplectic and used the media as an instrument for his vitriol, a practice he continues to this day, and for which I have had to retain a cadre of attorneys to protect Farrah's memory and what's left of my once good name. Someone would actually call the police. I still don't know who. And next thing I know, there would be an investigation of "elder abuse," that an infirm old woman was coerced into letting me control the project. I never told Farrah that the word "elder" was used. She'd have sweet-talked her doctor into surgically removing that someone's unholy tongue.

By April 2009, Redmond is in prison, having exhausted the court's willingness to give him another chance. Though it was heavily covered in the press, by then Farrah was too weak to read the papers herself, and so I would cut out the articles I thought she'd enjoy and read them to her. I made

sure she never saw a word about Redmond's incarceration.
I told her the reason he wasn't able to visit was because he
was in rehab.

JOURNAL ENTRY, APRIL 13, 2009
Farrah is drugged into a constant sleep. I miss her so
much and she's just in the next room. She asked me
today, "Am I going to make it?" I told her, "Of course
you're going to make it, and if not, I'm going with
you." She smiled and drifted off.

JOURNAL ENTRY, APRIL 30, 2009
I lay next to her in bed and hold her, thinking to
myself, haven't I done this somewhere before? She
asks me in a voice that has become barely a whisper,
must she get another procedure? I promise her
"no more."

JOURNAL ENTRY, MAY 4, 2009
I slept in her bed last night but I'm not sure she knew
I was there. I kissed her nose, her chin, her forehead,
whispering over and over how much I love her.

It was during this period that Farrah would see her son
for the last time. If you've seen the documentary, it's not easy
to forget the scene in which Redmond, his feet in shackles, is
led into his mother's bedroom, where he lays his head on her

chest, telling her how much she means to him. As I watched him clinging to his dying mother, a thousand and one snapshots flicked across my memory: Farrah tickling her redheaded toddler as he giggled with glee; little Redmond and his mom snuggled under the covers singing "Who's Afraid of the Big Bad Wolf"; Farrah running with her son on the beach, Davey Dog barking and wagging his tail behind them; a long, lean adolescent Redmond shooting hoops with Farrah in the driveway on Antelo. I ached for them both, but especially for Redmond. That final visit with his mom had to have been hard for him in ways you or I can't imagine.

On May 15 of 2009, *Farrah's Story* aired on NBC. It will be nominated for an Emmy. We watched it together that night. Farrah couldn't sit up on her own anymore, so I sat beside her and she leaned on me for support. She compliments the Van Morrison score, teases me by asking who supervised the brilliant editing. Her body is dying while her hydrangea-blue eyes are alight with fierce satisfaction. I will ask her to marry me again and she'll accept. I'll buy the ring. The priest at St. John's Hospital will come to marry us and administer last rights instead.

After the priest leaves, I move the cot I'd been sleeping on these past days away from the bed, lie down next to her, wrap my body around her to keep her warm, and then take her hand. I can feel a steady pulse. Her oncologist Dr. Piro comes into the room and says, "I had hoped I would never have to say this, but I think we should let her go."

"We need some time," I say. And Dr. Piro leaves us alone. I caress her hand for hours. Her heart refuses to quit. I feel someone patting my shoulder. Dr. Piro's whisper tells me, "It's time to remove the IV; the nourishment is just feeding the cancer. There is no possibility of recovery anymore." I watch a nurse take the needle out of Farrah's arm, and she's careful to put a Band-Aid over the puncture just as she would with a healthy patient. I can hear the wheels of the IV stand being rolled out of the room. Dr. Piro says to me, "It may take some time and I know you want to stay with her." I'm left alone with my love. I take her hand. I can still feel her pulse, but now it is fluttering. She's trying to let go. Her heartbeat slows, then disappears. On the morning of June 25, Farrah slips into eternal sleep.

I don't remember that long walk down the corridor as I made my way out of the hospital. All I recall is being accosted by media the moment I stepped outside. I can still hear the clicking of flashbulbs, and a hundred questions being hurled at me from all sides. I push my way through and get into my car. I'm in a daze. I can't think. I go to her condo on Wilshire. I walk into the bedroom and lie on the cool, crisp sheets. Draped across a chair are a pair of jeans and a T-shirt, probably her outfit for a next morning that never came. Her hairbrush is sitting on the dresser, strands of her exquisite golden locks reflecting from the sunlight streaming in through the window. It's as if she's still there and will be breezing in at any moment. I close my eyes and

gather my courage for the phone call that I'm so terribly reluctant to make but know I must. I dial the prison where
Redmond is incarcerated. I ask for the chaplain, who then
brings Red to the phone. I tell him that his mom is gone.
He's silent for a moment, and then I hear a sob. I ache that
I'm not there with him, but visiting day is on Sunday and by
then Farrah's passing will have been all over the media and
I didn't want our son to learn of his mother's death from a
radio broadcast or a television news show, or a guard.

JOURNAL ENTRY, JUNE 30, 2009
Dear one, this is it, the day I prayed would never
come. Maybe you're perched up high in the rafter
listening to your Mass. The last Mass we will share
together. It should have been me. We both know
that, don't we? I've written almost thirty years
continually about us. I'll never stop. I hope you know
that I beg your forgiveness. I never deserved you, but
there wasn't a day I didn't love you.

In the days and weeks following Farrah's death, some
of the journalists who had been cruel to my family in
the past crossed the line into the perverse. *Vanity Fair*
suggested the unthinkable, that I had come on to my own
daughter. It was an innocent private joke between Tatum
and me. The only people in the world who understood its

context were the two of us. Ever since she was a little girl, Tatum and I would play this game pretending we'd just met. It was silly and sweet. So at the funeral I greeted her with my line from our little act to let her know how much I loved her and that I still remembered, despite the difficulties between us. I was worried she'd feel uncomfortable at the funeral and I wanted to try to make her smile, if only for a moment. Someone apparently overheard me and said I didn't recognize my own daughter. *Vanity Fair* twisted the incident to enhance an already scathing story. And when the press asked Tatum about it, instead of contradicting the magazine's version, she fed the fire. It was humiliating, but what hurt most was that my daughter would let the media turn something cherished between us into a tawdry headline without a second thought. I considered trying to set the record straight myself, but I didn't think anyone would believe me.

Then Griffin would appear on *Larry King Live* for a final bravado performance, the same old lies, just different names and dates. He can no longer make me angry, only sad.

As the months passed and the tide of media coverage began to recede, I just wanted to hide away at the beach house and mourn in peace. But I had Redmond, who needed me desperately, and I was under contract for *Bones*. And Farrah would be furious with me if I let the ache of losing her dilute my spirit. I had let her down too often when she was alive. I couldn't again now that she was gone. I de-

cided to write this book both as a tribute to Farrah and to
honor our life together. I didn't expect I'd open up the way
that I have in these pages, but the further I got into the research and writing, the more I realized I needed to tell the
full story, not some fairy-tale version that wouldn't have the
richness of the truth.

Red and I, trying to hold it together in the
wake of the greatest loss of our lives.

That's why I've included the document below. I didn't
come across it until I was more than halfway through the
book. It's in Farrah's handwriting, scribbled across the mar-
gins of one of my journal entries, which I wrote before going
to sleep on the night that she caught me with Leslie. She must
have written it only days later when she was at the beach
house packing up her things or maybe picking up Redmond.

JOURNAL ENTRY, THE MORNING OF FEBRUARY 18, 1997

Kind of a long day so far, starting with my car phone going off with the unsmiling Ms. Fawcett about my not calling her back last night. So what do I say? Once a man has been tossed out of the game of love, the rules don't apply anymore.

Farrah writing in my journal, February 18, 1997:

Aren't you going to write about January 18, 1997, 1:42 a.m.? . . .

She was so upset that she got the date wrong. It was *February 18*.

. . . I'm still in shock and overcome with such sadness. I see my love, my life going away and you said it was forever. I do apologize. I feel so pitiful and disgraced, forgive my intrusion. Just know that I want you to be happy, but I doubt I ever will be again. Living without you is one thing, you leaving and living with beauty all around causes an ache I've never known. I will miss you. I guess I did really love you and sensed I was losing you. I'm sorry. I just needed to talk to you. I'm sorry my love. I've backed all the way up, I promise. She's

really beautiful of body and face. You're very lucky.
But so is she. —F.

Maybe if I had seen her note the day she wrote it, maybe
if I had never gotten involved with Leslie, if, if, if . . . I lament the years we wasted because this note remained hidden. Why couldn't I have found it before she died so I could
have told her that if I had to do it all over again, I would do
everything differently!

I'm sitting in my bedroom in Malibu, watching a movie I
last saw twenty-five years ago. The moon's light reflects
off the ocean and through my windows. I'm rapt, sometimes
shaking my head, amused, other times saluting the actors for
a scene that is fully convincing. I'm not blind to the obvious
ironies, the occasional triteness, but the depth of meaning is
inescapable. There is good reason all those girls and women
cried before their jaded friends told them they had been
manipulated. There is a reason *Love Story* remains one of
the most popular movies ever: while premature death may
be a dramatic cliché, it is also half of all human unhappiness. That is why a generation wept, and why after losing
my mate too soon, I will not go into that long good night
without a fight.

Farrah Fawcett

February 2, 1947 - June 25, 2009

My dazzling girl. This shot, used in the program at her memorial, captures her love of life.

POSTSCRIPT

Before Farrah died, she created the Farrah Fawcett Foundation, currently administered by Alana Stewart, her longtime friend and colleague. The Farrah Fawcett Foundation's mission is to provide funding for alternative methods of cancer research.

Tatum and I continue to struggle toward the light.

Redmond lives his life one day at a time.

Patrick is entering his twelfth year as a sportscaster with Fox Sports West and Prime Ticket.

I wish Griffin well.

ACKNOWLEDGMENTS

This book would never have been possible without the care, support, and faith of the following people:

David Pinsky, Keith Sunde, Alexandra Ferick, Stephanie Lynn, Mela Murphy, Alana Stewart, Dr. Annie Harvilicz, Bernie Francis, Kim Swartz and his wife, Megan Blake, Sylvia and Tommy Dorsey, Marcia Packard, Patrick O'Neal, the staff at the Malibu Beach Inn, Dee Salinas, Melissa Skolek, Dr. Lawrence Piro, Arnold Robinson—and Mozart.

And special thanks to Nan Talese.

And also Suzanne O'Neill and Tina Constable, my editor and my publisher at Crown Archetype.

Also thanks to the rest of the Archetype team: Anna Thompson, Campbell Wharton, Tammy Blake, Meredith McGinnis, Cindy Berman, Laura Duffy, Kevin Garcia, and Barbara Sturman.

And, of course, my coauthors, Jodee Blanco and Kent Carroll.